Success! Passing the Numeracy Skills Test for Teachers

CRITICAL
LEARNING

Success!
Passing the Numeracy
Skills Test for Teachers

JENNY LAWSON & TRISH KREFT

CRITICAL LEARNING

First published in 2017 by Critical Publishing Ltd

British Library Cataloguing in Publication Data
A CIP record for this book is available from the British Library

ISBN: 978-1-911106-87-6

This book is also available in the following e-book formats:

MOBI ISBN: 978-1-911106-88-3
EPUB ISBN: 978-1-911106-89-0
Adobe e-book ISBN: 978-1-911106-90-6

Cover and text design by Out of House Design
Project Management by Out of House Publishing
Printed and bound in Great Britain by 4edge, Essex

Critical Publishing
3 Connaught Road
St Albans
AL3 5RX

www.criticalpublishing.com

Printed on FSC accredited paper

Contents

Meet the authors

Hi, I'm Jenny Lawson.

As a long-standing member of the AlphaPlus Consultancy, I have devised many online tests for trainee teachers. Alongside my teaching and examining career, I have authored, and been the series editor for, numerous texts for ICT and mathematics, from Key Stage 1 through to A level and GNVQ. Now retired from full-time teaching, I focus on my own writing and also offer mentoring for writers wanting to be published.

I'm Trish Kreft.

I have over 35 years' experience of teaching and managing mathematics and teacher education in a variety of settings, including schools, further education, adult and community learning and university. Since 2006, I have been running my own training company as well as working as an independent consultant in mathematics teacher education, guidance and quality assurance.

Introduction

How the book is structured

This book starts with an initial section on 'Preparation and planning: your career path into teaching' and an overview of 'The Professional Skills Tests'.

The numeracy section is then presented as a series of topics: number, measure, statistics, presentation of data and algebra. For each topic, the essential knowledge is given, with examples followed by practice questions – 212 in all.

At the end of the numeracy section, there are four practice papers.

At the back of the book, there are answers to all questions and a 'Show me' section with the working for every question explained.

Finally, there is a numeracy glossary, a list of acronyms and useful websites plus a comprehensive index.

How to use the information in this book

Do the online practice tests to identify your strengths and weaknesses.

For your weakest topics, study the notes and examples, and try the practice questions. If you answer a question incorrectly, read the 'Show me' explanation.

Only when you feel you have grasped the techniques involved for one topic should you move on to the next topic; and so on, until you have revised all necessary topics.

Now try a practice paper or two. For any incorrect answers, work out where you are going wrong. Read back over any relevant theory.

Go back and try another online test.

Repeat until you are confident you will pass the skills test!

Why you need it

Ideally, you need to pass first time. If you don't, you may not be offered a place on an Initial Teacher Training (ITT) course.

If you don't pass first time, you can pay for two more attempts. If you fail all three attempts, you have to wait two years before you can have another go and then start your course.

Overview of the book features

You'll see a number of icons in the margins of the book and some recurring headings. These might occur anywhere and highlight particular activities or important information.

KEY POINT: draws your attention to a really important point within the text.

GO ONLINE: directs you to search for online sources of information.

LOOK IT UP: directs you to a hard-copy source of information.

COMMON ERROR: highlights commonly made mistakes that you should be aware of and seek to avoid.

FREQUENTLY ASKED QUESTION: highlights common questions.

GLOSSARY ITEM: any words that are defined in the glossary are highlighted in bold on their first appearance in the text, which might sometimes be in a heading, and are further signalled by the glossary icon in the margin. The glossary can be found at the back of the book.

CALCULATOR ALLOWED: this shows that you can use a calculator for the next and any subsequent numeracy questions.

CALCULATOR NOT ALLOWED: this indicates that you are not allowed to use a calculator for the next and any subsequent numeracy questions.

TRY THIS: this heading signals an exercise for you to try that relates specifically to the text you have just read or the section you are working through. The end of the example is also clearly indicated.

PRACTICE QUESTIONS: this heading is used before a batch of practice questions, in the same format as test questions, that relate to the section of text you have just read.

EXAMPLE: used for worked examples in the numeracy section of the book.

Full PRACTICE PAPERS appear at the end of part three and have a tint behind them so you can easily spot them.

A boxed feature identifies the ANSWERS to all the practice questions and the practice papers at the back of the book and the SHOW ME section of the answers gives you the detailed working for all the answers to the numeracy practice questions and practice papers.

1 Preparation and planning: your career path into teaching

If you are interested in becoming a teacher, visit the Get Into Teaching website at www.education.gov.uk/get-into-teaching.

Register with Get Into Teaching for personalised support and advice.

Routes into teaching

To achieve qualified teacher status (QTS), some form of teacher training has to be completed. Initial Teacher Training (ITT) routes depend on what age range you want to teach, whether you want to specialise in any particular subject(s), any previous experience and your existing qualifications.

Assessment only (AO)	For experienced teachers with a degree who have not yet achieved QTS Assessed in a school May not need further training
School-centred initial teacher training (SCITT)	Learn on the job Work as part of a teaching team during training Duration: 1 year End qualification: PGCE and/or master's-level credits
University-led training	For graduates and undergraduates Based in a university, but with at least two school placements End qualification: PGCE
Teach First	For outstanding graduates Earn while you train Work in a challenging school in a low-income community Duration: 2 years

Researchers in Schools (RIS)	For academics who have completed (or are finishing) a doctorate Salaried programme School-based in non-selective state schools Duration: 2 years
School Direct	For graduates who have been working for 3 years Train while working in a school Salaried programme May include PGCE qualification
Troops to Teachers	For ex-service personnel

Whichever route is taken, ITT includes an element of academic study, at least 24 weeks in at least two schools gaining practical classroom experience, and assessment by classroom observation.

School structure

Year	Age	School	Key Stage	Examinations
Nursery	3–4		Early Years Foundation Stage (EYFS)	
Reception	4–5	Infant or primary		
1	5–6		KS1	
2	6–7			SATs
3	7–8	Junior or primary	KS2	
4	8–9			
5	9–10			
6	10–11			SATs
7	11–12	Secondary	KS3	
8	12–13			
9	13–14			SATs
10	14–15		KS4	
11	15–16			GCSE
12	16–17	Secondary or sixth-form college	KS5	
13	17–18			A level, BTEC, etc

What qualifications do you need to enter ITT?

Required qualifications depend on the age group you want to teach: primary or secondary.

Qualification	Primary	Secondary
Professional Skills Tests (literacy and numeracy)	✓	✓
GCSE grade C or equivalent in mathematics	✓	✓
GCSE grade C or equivalent in English	✓	✓
GCSE grade C or equivalent in science	✓	
A degree	✓	
A degree relevant to the subject to be taught OR attendance on an SKE (subject knowledge enhancement) course		✓

If you don't have a degree and want to teach mathematics, computing, physics, chemistry, languages or design and technology, the ITT provider may offer you a subject knowledge enhancement (SKE) course as part of the selection process.

Bursaries may also be available for these SKE courses, depending on the length of the course.

Find out more about SKE – search for the SKE course directory.

Classroom experience is also recommended and will strengthen your application.

If you hope to teach a secondary subject, the School Experience Programme (SEP), run by the National College for Teaching and Leadership (NCTL), offers placements providing opportunities to observe teaching and pastoral work, to talk to teachers and to plan and deliver part or all of a lesson.

If you are interested in teaching at primary level, one way to gain classroom experience is to organise it yourself though local contacts, or by using the EduBase portal, which lists all educational establishments in England and Wales.

Go to the EduBase portal and identify all schools within a 25-mile radius of your home.

The Get Into Teaching website at www.education.gov.uk/get-into-teaching offers good advice on how to secure classroom experience.

What qualities do I need?

- A deep understanding of and enthusiasm for your own subject
- Commitment
- A positive attitude towards working with children
- Advanced communication and interpersonal skills
- Energy, enthusiasm and patience

2 The Professional Skills Tests

You will need to pass both the literacy and the numeracy skills tests. Gaining a pass in these Professional Skills Tests is a prerequisite if you want to embark on Initial Teacher Training (ITT); the tests have to be taken – and passed – ahead of the start of ITT.

Details of candidates' bookings, the number of attempts and scores are recorded on a computerised online booking system and this information is made available to ITT providers. ITT providers may then use the results of the tests to inform their decisions as to which applicants are offered places on an ITT course.

Failing to pass first time can adversely affect your prospects of gaining a place on an ITT course.

This is the recommended process.

○ Book a test appointment at a nearby test centre.
○ Submit an ITT application.
○ Prepare for the tests.
○ Take the tests.
○ Attend the ITT interview with test results.

There are a limited number of places on ITT courses so try to pass the Professional Skills Tests first time, and – to avoid disappointment – to schedule them well ahead of the start of your ITT course.

Passing the tests first time is the least expensive and quickest route. So, success is essential, and the key to success is in the preparation for the tests.

Who has to take the tests?

All applicants for ITT courses, including early years teacher courses, are required to pass the Professional Skills Tests before commencing their course.

Applicants who haven't passed the tests, even if offered a conditional place, will not be allowed to start their course.

Booking the test

The appointments for the Professional Skills Tests are booked through learndirect. First, you need to register with learndirect. All contact with learndirect is via email, so you need a valid email address.

The information you enter on the registration forms online must match the documents you will present as proof of ID at the test centre. If they don't match, you will not be permitted to take the test on that occasion.

Having registered, you can access your details, book tests, manage your appointments and view any results.

Having booked a test appointment, you may cancel or reschedule, provided you give at least three working days' notice.

If you are unwell, think ahead to your test booking and consider rescheduling.

Where to take the tests and what to expect

Tests are taken at a test centre.

When booking the tests, choose the most convenient test centre for you.

The visit will be for approximately 90 minutes, or longer if you have requested – and been granted – additional test time.

The test centre will have a waiting area with drinking water available, free of charge, plus toilet facilities that you can use before or after the test.

On arrival, you will be given an information sheet to read, which explains the procedure.

A copy of the information sheet is available for download from the Department for Education (DfE) website at www.education.gov.uk/sta/professional.

The next step is validation. Your identity will be checked against the details provided when you registered for the test. Forms of identification and evidence as specified on the registration form must be provided.

If you fail to provide all that is required, you will not be permitted to take the test. The fee for the test is forfeited and another date will need to be booked. Since there is a deadline for the test, this could jeopardise your prospects of starting the ITT course.

If all the necessary paperwork is in order, the test supervisor will allocate a locker key. Everything – apart from your primary form of ID and the locker key – has to be put into the locker for the duration of the test. This includes mobile phones and other electronic devices and personal items such as outdoor clothing, money, food and drink.

Eating and smoking is not permitted in the test room. No paperwork other than the primary ID is allowed in the test room: no pens, dictionaries, revision notes or books.

If you intend to retain any head covering, the test supervisor may ask you to remove the head covering so that you can be searched to ensure you have not secreted a Bluetooth device on your person. This can be done in a private area if you prefer, and this option should be requested during the validation stage.

Only once all your belongings are securely locked away, and the test supervisor is content that you have nothing that could be used to help you in the test, will you be escorted to the test room. Other candidates will already be midway through their tests, so silence must be observed on entering the room, and throughout the test.

Each candidate is allocated a workstation. Your primary ID will be checked again, and the supervisor will ensure the workstation is set up for the test you have booked. You can then start!

When you have completed the test, you should return to the locker to collect your personal belongings and then return the locker key to reception.

You will be asked to complete a short customer satisfaction survey; this is optional but feedback is always appreciated.

The test result is only available during this visit to the test centre, so you will need to wait until it is available. All tests are computer marked and a printed score report is provided.

 There is no certificate; this printed score report is your proof that you have passed (or not!). Keep it safe.

 If you leave the test centre without collecting the score report, you will have to rebook and pay for another test.

Test results are also uploaded to your account on the booking system within 48 hours of the test. If you don't pass the test you will have to wait until the result is uploaded before you can book a re-sit.

Number of attempts

You are only allowed three attempts, and then have to wait two years (24 months from the date of the second re-sit) before you are allowed to try again.

Costs

The first attempt at each test is free of charge. If the first test is rescheduled, as long as it is more than three days before the test date, is still free of charge. The second and any subsequent tests are not free of charge. Currently, the price is £19.25 per test.

Payment is by credit/debit card at the time of booking. Provided sufficient notice is given, fees for cancelled appointments are refunded, and the monies should be received within ten working days.

For how long are the tests valid?

Test passes remain valid for three years. If you apply for an ITT course which starts after the end of the three-year period, you have to re-sit the test(s).

Special arrangements

In accordance with the Equalities Act 2010, special arrangements may be requested if you have a documented medical condition or disability that would adversely affect your performance in the test.

- Extra time may be granted for those with specific learning difficulties such as dyslexia.
- A modified version of the literacy test may be given to candidates with a hearing impairment. The audio spelling test is replaced by an onscreen multiple-choice format.
- A modified version of the numeracy test may be given to candidates with a hearing impairment. The audio mental arithmetic test is supplemented by onscreen multiple-choice format questions.
- Candidates with physical disabilities may be given extra time. They may be allowed to bring specialist equipment with them to the test centre.
- Candidates with visual impairment may be allocated a larger monitor screen and/or large-print hard copies of the test. They may also be allocated more time.
- Candidates for whom English is not their first language may request extra time and/or the option to listen to an audio version of the question, to accompany the onscreen instructions.

Full details of what is possible are given on the DfE website.

If you require special arrangements to be made, you have to request these and provide proof of your physical/educational circumstances.

Facilities vary from test centre to test centre. The majority of test centres are fully accessible but, if you require special facilities, you should check beforehand that the test centre you have requested will be suitable.

Some special arrangements can be made via the online booking system; for some, an application form has to be completed. A response should be received within ten working days but more complex applications can take longer.

Preparation for the tests

Apart from making sure you understand the theory on which you will be tested, before taking the real tests, it's important to take the online practice tests.

Details of the current technical requirements to gain access to the tests are provided on the DfE website. Most operating systems and browsers are supported.

Completing the practice questions and the practice papers provided in this book will reassure you that you can answer the questions correctly and earn marks, but it cannot prepare you fully for the onscreen tests.

The online tests provide essential experience and practice in using the navigational features of the test, including how to:

- enter an answer;
- use the calculator;

○   edit an answer;

○   flag a question – so you can remember to go back to it, if you have time;

○   proceed to the next question;

○   end the test, if you have finished before the time runs out.

Entering an answer can be done via the keyboard, by dragging the answer or one or more ticks into place, or clicking on the answer. Full instructions are always given on screen.

Doing the online tests also familiarises you with other features.

○   A clock shows how much time has elapsed.

○   A question track shows which questions you have answered so far – clicking on a question number allows you to go back to that question.

Note that there is a 'Help' button in the practice tests, and a 'Pause' button. Neither is available in the real tests!

The onscreen test facility checks your answers, gives a total score and reports on which questions you answered incorrectly, together with the expected answer. In the numeracy tests, there is also an option to work through a question using step-by-step support. The 'Show me' option gives the correct working so you can see where you went wrong.

 Before gaining access to the tests, you will need to complete an initial registration with learndirect. Full details are provided on the DfE website at www.education.gov.uk/sta/professional, with links to the form that has to be completed.

 Copy the activation key so you can paste it into the registration form. It is an easily mistyped combination of letters, for example jhULiqgX.

The numeracy skills test

In the numeracy test, unless special arrangements have been made, you have 48 minutes to answer 28 questions, and these are split into two sections:

○   12 mental arithmetic questions;

○   16 written questions for which an onscreen calculator is provided.

During the first mental arithmetic section, each question is presented via headphones and is individually timed. You can make notes and work out your answer on paper before entering it on screen.

Then, in the calculator section, the 16 questions test two aspects of numeracy:

○   7 questions test three aspects of 'interpreting and using written data';

○   9 questions require the solution to a 'written arithmetic problem'.

The first 12 (mental) questions and the final 9 (calculator) questions test the topics listed in the table on page 11.

The numeracy skills test does not test your knowledge of the mathematics national curriculum, nor your ability to teach mathematics.

The middle 7 questions can also test skills from throughout the topic list but are primarily designed to test your ability to interpret and use written data to:

o   identify trends;

o   make comparisons in order to draw conclusions;

o   interpret information.

Topics tested in the first 12 and final 9 questions	Mental arithmetic	Arithmetic problems	Page numbers
Time	✓	✓	30
Amounts of money	✓	✓	27
Proportion involving fractions	✓	✓	14, 24
Proportion involving percentages	✓	✓	20, 24
Proportion involving decimals	✓	✓	17, 24
Ratios		✓	25
Percentages in various contexts	✓	✓	20
Fractions	✓	✓	14
Decimals	✓	✓	17
Measurements involving distance	✓	✓	32
Measurements involving area	✓	✓	33
Measurements involving other measures, eg volume	✓		35
Conversions from one currency to another	✓	✓	29
Conversions from fractions to decimals	✓	✓	19
Conversions from decimals to fractions	✓	✓	18
Conversions involving other measures		✓	36
Averages: mean		✓	39
Averages: median		✓	41
Averages: mode		✓	43
Range		✓	44
Combinations of measures of average		✓	46
Using simple formulae		✓	87

All 28 questions carry one mark regardless of the number of responses required.

❷ FAQs

Q: In the numeracy test, if all questions carry one mark regardless of the number of required responses, surely some tests will be harder to pass than others?

A: No two tests can ever be the same. However, to ensure candidates are treated equally, regardless of which test they take, the numeracy skills tests have been calibrated statistically against a benchmark test. Therefore, a test with slightly harder questions is given a slightly lower pass mark and a test with slightly easier questions is given a slightly higher pass mark.

Types of response

In the audio/mental section, an answer box appears into which to enter the answer.

For the onscreen section, there are several different types of response.

- With the multiple-choice questions, a range of answers is presented, only one of which is the correct answer.
- With a single-response answer, as with the audio section, you will see an answer box into which you enter the answer.
- With the multiple-response type, there is only one mark but you have to give several answers. These may be statements that you have to classify as true or not true.
- For some questions, you need to select answers and place them in the correct position.
- For some, you point and click on the correct answer.

Do the online practice tests to become familiar with the different types of response strategy.

> The textual nature of this book offers no opportunity for such technological variety, so the practice questions, and the questions in the practice papers, are worded as if they were on screen, with additional numbering/lettering applied for ease of cross-referencing with the answers.

Top tips for the numeracy skills test

Answers, when entered using the keyboard, are as a number, not in words.

Units are always provided (eg eggs, %) so only the number has to be entered.

Only digits are allowed, with a decimal point if needed. No additional spaces or characters should be entered, just the number.

If you enter 2cm instead of 2, you will not earn the mark.

No leading zeroes should be entered.

If you enter 0125 instead of 125, you will not earn the mark.

Tips for the audio section

Each question is read aloud twice, so you have time to understand what is required.

The first time you hear a question, jot down the numbers involved. Listen also for key words which tell you what operation is needed: add, subtract, multiply or divide.

Start working out the answer as soon as you have enough information.

During the second reading of the question, listen for special instructions such as the level of **accuracy**, or the format to be used for questions involving time.

A fixed time is allowed and it should be long enough for you to do the calculation, before the next question is read to you. However, be aware of strategies that save you time:

$5 \times £1.99 = 5 \times (£2 - 1p) = £10 - 5p = £9.95$.

Note that fractions must be entered in the lowest terms.

If you run out of time, guess an answer; that's better than not putting anything.

Tips for the onscreen section

The numeracy syllabus includes many topics. Some you might find easy, others not so. To maximise your score in the test, don't waste time on a question that looks difficult to you. Answer the easiest questions first. You can always go back, if you have time, and fill in the gaps.

All the information needed to work out an answer is given in a question. Read the question twice before starting to answer it, to locate the essential data.

Check the stem of the question carefully. You won't need to spend time – and risk making a mistake – in counting the number of data items, or points on a scatter graph, if that information is already provided in the stem.

Remember that you don't have to get every question right to pass. Just do your best!

3 Numeracy skills

This section introduces all the terminology, and explains all the techniques and methods, needed to pass the numeracy test.

The topics are introduced through the general areas of number, measure, statistics, presentation of data and algebra, with examples and practice questions for each topic, and then four practice papers covering all topics.

3.1 Number

This section introduces fractions, decimals and percentages, and how to convert between them. Fractions, decimals and percentages may also be tested within other more complex topics. The LOOK IT UP feature points ahead to the more challenging practice questions.

Fractions

Fractions like $\frac{1}{2}$ and $\frac{1}{5}$ are equal parts of a whole. Halve a pint of milk and you get $\frac{1}{2}$ a pint of milk.

Divide a bar of chocolate between five people, and each person gets $\frac{1}{5}$ of the bar.

The number of the top (**numerator**) is what you started with (1 whole). The number on the bottom (**denominator**) is how many equal parts resulted from the sharing.

As with whole numbers, you can count with fractions.

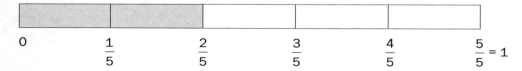

$\frac{2}{5}$ can be thought of as $\frac{1}{5} + \frac{1}{5} = 2 \times \frac{1}{5}$.

It's also the same as $2 \div 5$.

Simplest form/lowest terms

Multiplying (or dividing) both the top and bottom of a fraction by the same number does not change the fraction. It creates families of equivalent fractions.

$$\frac{1}{2} = \frac{2}{4} \qquad\qquad \frac{1}{5} = \frac{2}{10} = \frac{3}{15} \qquad\qquad \frac{2}{3} = \frac{4}{6} = \frac{6}{9}$$

A fraction that cannot be divided – when there is no common **factor** in the numerator and denominator – is called the **lowest term** – or simplest term.

To simplify a fraction, think of a number which divides exactly into both top and bottom. Do the division and repeat until there is no number which divides exactly into top and bottom numbers.

Example

In a class of twenty-four, six children go home for lunch. What fraction goes home for lunch?

$$6 \text{ out of } 24 = \frac{6}{24}$$

Always give the answer in the lowest terms.

6 and 24 are both even numbers, divisible by 2.

Dividing top and bottom by 2:

$$\frac{6}{24} = \frac{3}{12}$$

12 and 3 are both divisible by 3:

$$\frac{3}{12} = \frac{1}{4}$$

Answer: One-quarter of the children go home for lunch.

Practice questions

1   A student scores fourteen out of thirty in a test. What fraction is this in its lowest form?

2   The Year 6 teacher examined the performance of her pupils at the end of Year 5.

Level	1	2	3	4	5
Boys	2	3	4	5	1
Girls	0	2	5	6	0

What fraction of the boys is above level 2 and below level 5? Give your answer in its lowest terms.

3   In a Year 11 group, $\frac{5}{8}$ are taking part in either a sponsored walk or a sponsored swim. Of those taking part, ¼ have chosen to do the sponsored swim. What fraction of the whole year group is taking part in a sponsored swim? Give your answer as a fraction in its lowest terms.

Fractions of amounts

To calculate a fraction of an amount, multiply the amount by the fraction.

$$\frac{1}{2} \text{ of £56} = \frac{1}{2} \times \text{£56}$$

'Of' means multiply in fractions and percentages.

To calculate <u>mentally</u> the fraction of an amount, first share by the denominator, and then multiply by the numerator.

Example

Two-thirds of the pupils in class 6B bring sandwiches for lunch. There are 33 in the class. How many bring a packed lunch?

To find ⅔ of a number, first find ⅓ and then double your answer.

$$\frac{1}{3} \text{ of 33} = 33 \div 3 = 11$$

$$\frac{2}{3} \text{ of 33} = 2 \times 11 = 22$$

Answer: 22 pupils bring a packed lunch.

<u>Using a calculator</u>, since the order of operations is immaterial for multiplication and division, multiply by the numerator and then divide by the denominator.

Example

Three-fifths of the pupils in class 6C have school dinners. There are thirty-five in the class. How many have school dinners?

$$\frac{3}{5} \text{ of 35} = \frac{3}{5} \times 35$$

Calculate: $35 \times 3 \div 5 = 21$

Answer: 21 have school dinners.

Another way of dividing by 5 is to divide by 10 and then double the answer.

Practice questions

4   Two-thirds of three hundred and forty-two pupils have a hot school meal. How many pupils in total have a hot school meal?

5   A school has two hundred and eighty-eight pupils. Three-eighths of the pupils are eligible for free school meals. How many pupils are eligible for free school meals?

6   In a class of twenty-seven pupils, four out of nine are girls. How many are boys?

7   There are one hundred and eighty pupils in a primary school. Forty-five of these are in the Reception class. What fraction is this of the whole?

8   After heavy snowfall, one-third of the pupils are not able to attend their primary school on that day. The total number of pupils on the school roll is three hundred and fifty-four. How many pupils did attend that day?

9   Year 3 pupils carried out a survey into the pets they each had at home. A quarter of the pupils in Year 3 had a cat and one-third of those with a cat also had a dog. There are 48 pupils in Year 3. What fraction of the Year 3 pupils had a cat and a dog? Give your answer as a fraction in its lowest terms.

For more practice questions testing your knowledge of fractions, see practice questions 14–17, 19–20, 22–23, 38–39, 46–47, 62, 69, 123, 125, 128, 147, 149, 155, 178, 189.

Decimals

Decimals are numbers with a decimal point, which indicates where the whole number part ends and the fractional part starts.

In the decimal system, the value of a digit depends on where it is placed in a number.

In 176.95, the **place value** of the 9 is nine-tenths $\left(\frac{9}{10}\right)$ and the place value of the 5 is five-hundredths $\left(\frac{5}{100}\right)$.

H	T	U	.	t	h
1	7	6	.	9	5

Arithmetic can be performed on decimal numbers in the same way as for whole numbers.

Practice questions

10   What is nought point six of four hundred and twenty?

11   Nought point three of the pupils in one class of thirty pupils have extra music lessons. How many pupils in the class have extra music lessons?

12   Nought point seven of a year group of two hundred and ten pupils took part in a sponsored walk. How many did not take part?

13   In a schools' athletics competition, the 4-person relay team ran their legs with these times:

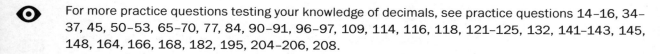

87.45 secs   78.92 secs   94.38 secs   72.1 secs

What was their combined time, in seconds?

For more practice questions testing your knowledge of decimals, see practice questions 14–16, 34–37, 45, 50–53, 65–70, 77, 84, 90–91, 96–97, 109, 114, 116, 118, 121–125, 132, 141–143, 145, 148, 164, 166, 168, 182, 195, 204–206, 208.

Conversions from fractions to decimals and vice versa, and rounding

To convert a decimal to a fraction, apply the place value for the digits after the decimal point.

$$0.1 = \frac{1}{10} \qquad 0.3 = \frac{3}{10} \qquad 0.7 = \frac{7}{10} \qquad 0.9 = \frac{9}{10} \qquad 0.01 = \frac{1}{100}$$

For factors of 10 (2 and 5) and 100 (25, 75), the fraction can be written in its lowest terms:

$$0.2 = \frac{2}{10} = \frac{1}{5} \qquad 0.25 = \frac{25}{100} = \frac{1}{4}$$

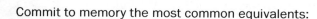

Commit to memory the most common equivalents:

$$0.5 = \frac{1}{2} \qquad 0.25 = \frac{1}{4} \qquad 0.75 = \frac{3}{4}.$$

Example

Of the total number of pupils in a school 0.85 have school dinners. Of those, 0.2 have special dietary requirements. What fraction of the total number of pupils in the school has school dinners and also has a special dietary requirement? Give your answer as a fraction in its lowest terms.

$$0.2 \times 0.85 = 0.17 = \frac{17}{100} \quad \text{OR} \quad 0.85 = \frac{85}{100} = \frac{17}{20}$$

$$0.2 = \frac{2}{10} = \frac{1}{5}$$

$$\frac{17}{20} \times \frac{1}{5} = \frac{17}{100}$$

Because a fraction represents a division – the numerator divided by the denominator – converting a fraction to its decimal equivalent is achieved by division.

Example

What is thirty-two out of forty as a decimal?

$$32 \text{ out of } 40 = \frac{32}{40} = \frac{16}{20} = \frac{8}{10} = 0.8$$

Answer: 32 out of 40 as a decimal is 0.8.

Practice questions

14   What is nought point six five as a fraction in its lowest terms?

15   Nought point four pupils in a school have free school meals. What is this as a fraction? Give your answer in its lowest terms.

16   At the end of Key Stage 2, nought point eight five pupils gained level four and above. What is this as a fraction? Give your answer in its lowest terms.

17   In Year 7 PE lessons, the teachers give the pupils a choice of sport. 0.4 selected football; 0.35 selected hockey and the rest selected netball or were excused PE that day. What fraction chose hockey? Give your answer in its lowest terms.

For more examples of practice questions testing your knowledge of converting from fractions to decimals and vice versa, see practice questions 34–37, 69, 97, 122, 125, 166, 168, 182.

A question may require an answer to be given to a certain number of decimal places, or the nearest whole number. With currency questions, this will usually be to the nearest penny – two decimal places for sterling amounts – or to the nearest pound.

Do not round your answer until the very end of a calculation.

Giving an answer 'to one decimal place' requires examination of the second decimal place and rounding up or down accordingly.

o   4.72 rounds to 4.7 because $\frac{2}{100} < \frac{5}{100}$

○ 4.75 rounds to 4.8 because convention rules that $\dfrac{5}{100}$ is to be rounded up.

○ 4.78 rounds to 4.8 because $\dfrac{8}{100} > \dfrac{5}{100}$

The same strategy applies, whatever the level of accuracy required: look at the next digit and round up/down according to that digit.

Depending on the context, it may be appropriate to round up/down, regardless of the place value of the digit to be rounded.

○ Sharing money or other items: rounding down is necessary. There will be a remainder that cannot be shared equally.

○ Sharing the cost: rounding up is necessary; otherwise there will be insufficient to pay the bill.

○ Deciding how many will fit within a space: rounding down is needed.

○ Determining, for example, how many coaches to hire for a school trip: rounding up will be necessary. This will mean spare seats but all children will be accommodated.

For questions that involve rounding see practice questions 24–28, 33, 35, 47, 49, 56, 58, 65–69, 84, 90–91, 94, 96–97, 118, 124, 126, 130–132, 134–135, 137–138, 140–141, 148, 150–151, 154, 162, 166, 168, 172, 177, 202–203, 206, 208.

Percentages

A percentage is an amount measured out of 100. The % symbol represents dividing by 100 or $\overline{100}$.

$$80\% = \dfrac{80}{100} = \dfrac{4}{5}$$

Commit to memory the most common percentages:

$10\% = \dfrac{1}{10}$ $12.5\% = \dfrac{1}{8}$ $20\% = \dfrac{1}{5}$

$25\% = \dfrac{1}{4}$ $50\% = \dfrac{1}{2}$ $75\% = \dfrac{3}{4}$

Notice that $100\% = \dfrac{100}{100} = 1$.

Example

Seven out of twenty-five pupils scored full marks in a test. What percentage of pupils scored full marks?

Replace 'out of' with a fraction line.

7 out of 25 means $\dfrac{7}{25}$.

There are four 25s in 100. Multiply top and bottom by 4 to get an equivalent fraction with 100 as the denominator.

$$\frac{7}{25} = \frac{28}{100} = 28\%$$

Answer: 28% of pupils scored full marks.

Practice questions

18   In a class of thirty pupils, forty per cent are boys. How many are girls?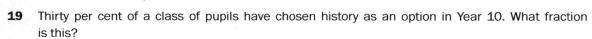

19   Thirty per cent of a class of pupils have chosen history as an option in Year 10. What fraction is this?

20   The local museum offers a discount of seventeen and a half per cent on admission prices for school groups. What fraction of the total admission price is this discounted rate? Give your answer as a fraction in its lowest form.

21   A test has forty-five questions, each worth one mark. The pass mark is seventy per cent. How many questions have to be answered correctly in order to gain a pass?

22   The pass mark for a test is set at sixty-five per cent. What fraction of the marks must a pupil obtain to pass? Give your answer as a fraction in its lowest form.

23   Fifty-five per cent of a class of twenty pupils are boys. What fraction are girls?

24   On one day in a high school, 2.5% of 960 pupils were absent, 15.2% were not in lessons because they were sitting exams and 5.3% were on a school trip. How many pupils were in lessons?

Converting decimals and fractions to percentages

○   To convert a decimal to a percentage, take the number of one-hundredths:

$$0.45 = \frac{45}{100} = 45\%$$

○   To convert a fraction into a percentage, multiply it by 100%. This does not change the size of the fraction, but gives it as a percentage.

$$\frac{3}{4} \times 100\% = 75\%$$

Don't 'multiply a fraction by 100' unless you want to make it 100 times bigger! Instead, multiply it by 100%.

Example

A student scores fifty-two out of a possible eighty in a test. What is this as a percentage?

$$52 \text{ out of } 80 = \frac{52}{80} = \frac{13}{20} = \frac{65}{100} = 65\%$$

Answer: 52 out of 80 as a percentage is 65%.

Practice questions

25   A pupil scores fourteen out of a possible forty-two marks. What is this as a percentage? Give your answer to the nearest whole number.

26   Twenty-seven hours a week are spent in lessons. The pupils in Year 10 have four and a half hours of mathematics per week. What percentage of the total is this? Give your answer to the nearest whole number.

27   Sixteen out of thirty pupils chose to take extra music lessons. What is this as a percentage? Give your answer to the nearest whole number.

28   Students have thirty hours of lessons per week, of which six hours are devoted to English. What percentage of the total weekly lesson time is devoted to English?

29   A pupil scores thirty-three out of sixty in a test. What is this as a percentage?

Percentages of amounts

'Of' means multiply in fractions and percentages.

A percentage is a fraction. To calculate the percentage of an amount, you have options:

○   Recognise the simple fractional equivalent of the percentage, and then calculate mentally as you would for a 'fraction of an amount' (page 16).

○   Revert to the $/_{100}$ form of the percentage, and then calculate using a calculator as you would for a 'fraction of an amount' (page 16).

Examples

In class 6D, forty per cent of the pupils wear glasses. There are thirty-five pupils in the class. How many pupils in class 6D wear glasses?

$$40\% = \frac{40}{100} = \frac{2}{5}$$

$\frac{1}{5}$ of 35 pupils = 7 pupils

$\frac{2}{5}$ of 35 pupils = 14 pupils

Answer: 14 pupils in class 6D wear glasses.

A supplier offers a 12.5% discount on orders over £100. The school orders £127 worth of books. What discount is given? Round down to the nearest 1p.

$$12.5\% \text{ of } £127 = \frac{12.5}{100} \times £127$$
$$= £127 \times 12.5 \div 100 = £15.875 = £15.88 \text{ to the nearest 1p.}$$

Answer: £15.88 discount is given.

Using a calculator, the £ sign is not entered, so it's important to be aware of the units of your answer.

A spring is 30 centimetres long. When stretched its length is increased by 25%. How long is the stretched spring?

$$25\% \text{ of } 30 = \frac{1}{4} \text{ of } 30 = 7.5$$

30cm + 7.5cm = 37.5cm

Answer: The stretched spring is 37.5cm long.

Don't just calculate the extension. Remember to add it to the original length to find the stretched length.

Practice questions

30 In a school of four hundred and twenty pupils, fifteen per cent receive free school meals. How many pupils do not receive free schools meals?

31 A sponsored spelling test raised sixty-five pounds, with forty-five per cent given to school funds and the remainder to charity. How much does the charity receive?

32 Seventy per cent of the cost of a school outing is subsidised. Pupils are asked to make a contribution of fifteen pounds each. What is the total cost per pupil?

Pupil	Actual age		Reading age	
	Years	Months	Years	Months
1	11	0	10	9
2	10	6	10	8
3	10	8	8	3
4	10	4	9	1
5	10	11	9	11
6	10	7	10	10

33 The reading ages of a group of Year 6 pupils receiving additional help was assessed.
Look at the table and indicate all the true statements:

A: Less than 80% of the pupils had a reading age below that of their actual age.

B: Pupil 3 had a 40% lower reading age compared to his actual age (to the nearest whole month).

C: 50% of the pupils had a reading age of at least 1 year 6 months below the actual age.

Percentage points

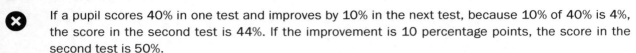

Comparing amounts given as raw data can be difficult. Are things getting better, or worse? Converting the raw data to percentages allows a direct comparison; an improvement can be measured in **percentage points**.

If a pupil scores 40% in one test and improves by 10% in the next test, because 10% of 40% is 4%, the score in the second test is 44%. If the improvement is 10 percentage points, the score in the second test is 50%.

Example

Twelve out of twenty Year 6 pupils are predicted level four in their mathematics Key Stage 2 test. Fifteen actually gained a level four. What is this, as a percentage points increase?

    12 out of 20 = 60%

    15 out of 20 = 75%

    75% − 60% = 15%

Answer: This is 15% as a percentage points increase.

For examples of questions that refer to percentages or percentage points, see practice questions 49, 63, 94, 98, 100, 109, 114, 119, 124, 127, 129, 131–132, 134–138, 141–143, 145, 149–156, 160–162, 169–172, 174–180, 182–184, 191–196, 198, 205–208.

Proportion involving fractions, percentages and decimals

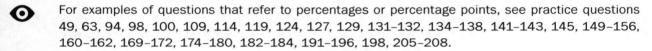

Proportion describes the relationship between some part of a whole, with the whole. It is usually expressed as a fraction, but can also be given as a percentage or as a decimal.

Example

In class 6D, there are thirty-five pupils and fourteen of them wear glasses. What proportion of class 6D wear glasses?

$$14 \text{ out of } 35 = \frac{14}{35} = \frac{2}{5} = 40\%$$

Answer: 40% of class 6D wear glasses.

Practice questions

34   Twenty-eight out of forty pupils in Year 6 achieved a level four or above in Key Stage 2 English. What proportion is this? Give your answer as a decimal.

35   In a survey of forty-eight pupils in Year 6 sixteen pupils stated that mathematics was their favourite subject. What proportion did not state that mathematics was their favourite subject? Give your answer as a decimal to two decimal places.

36   In a year group of one hundred and twenty-five pupils, seventy-five are boys. What proportion are boys? Give your answer as a decimal.

37   Seven out of twenty pupils in one class are absent with flu. What proportion is this as a decimal?

38   Pupils are studying weather patterns and record the midday temperature in °C over a period of five weeks in the winter.

°C	Mon	Tue	Wed	Thu	Fri
Week 1	−1	0	1	2	4
Week 2	3	2	−4	−3	−2
Week 3	2	2	1	0	0
Week 4	−3	−1	1	2	3
Week 5	4	0	0	−1	−4

What proportion of the total recordings was 0°C? Give your answer as a fraction in its lowest terms.

39   The Year 6 teacher examined the performance of her pupils at the end of Year 5.

Level	1	2	3	4	5
Boys	2	3	4	5	1
Girls	0	2	5	6	0

What proportion of pupils gained less than a level 4? Give your answer as a fraction in its lowest terms.

For more practice questions testing your knowledge of proportion, see practice questions 121–123, 125, 128, 132–133, 148, 155, 157–159, 168, 171, 182.

Ratios

Ratio describes the relationship between two parts of a whole. It is expressed using the : sign.

Example

In class 6E, there are 32 pupils. There are 18 girls. What is the ratio of boys to girls?

There are 18 girls.

32 − 18 = 14

There are 14 boys.

boys:girls = 14:18 = 7:9

Answer: The ratio is 7:9.

❌ The ordering of a ratio matters. 2:5 is not the same as 5:2.

Practice question

Year group	Boys	Girls
3	28	32
4	25	29
5	31	26
6	28	29

40   The table shows the gender breakdown in each year group of a junior school.

What is the ratio of boys to girls? Give your answer in its lowest terms.

👁 Ratios are also used in currency conversions and in map scales; see, for example, practice questions 40, 50–58, 70, 81, 87–88, 140.

3.2   Measure

Measure applies to money, time, length (or distance), area and volume. Calculation can be performed using measures just as they can with whole numbers and fractional quantities.

Money

The UK 'went decimal' in 1971 with 100p in £1. Prior to that, money was in pounds, shillings and pence.

Money is expressed using decimals. £1.50 means one pound and 0.5 of a pound.

Amounts of money

Cost is calculated using the formula: cost = quantity × price.

Examples

The school magazine sells for twenty pence per copy. At the school fete, one hundred and thirty-five copies were sold. How much money was collected?

$$135 \times 20p = 2700p = £27$$

Another way to multiply by 20p is to remember that 20p is $\frac{1}{5}$ of a pound.

$\frac{1}{5}$ of 100 = 20. $\frac{1}{5}$ of 35 = 7. $\frac{1}{5}$ of 135 = 27.

Answer: £27 was collected.

An educational visit will incur the following costs:

o   *£4.50 per pupil entry fee.*

o   *14 miles each way in three school minibuses, each costing 56p per mile.*

o   *Worksheets, costing £2.40 for a set of 30. Not available in smaller amounts.*

To go on the trip, 36 pupils have paid £6.50 each. What is the difference between the amount paid by the pupils and the total cost of the visit?

Work out the cost of each aspect of the visit: Entry: £4.50 × 36 = £162

Travel: 2 × 14 miles = 28 miles

28 × £0.56 × 3 = £47.04

Worksheets: 36 requires 2 sets

2 × £2.40 = £4.80

Calculate the total cost: £162 + £47.04 + £4.80 = £213.84

Calculate the contributions from pupils: 36 × £6.50 = £234

Calculate the difference: £234 − £213.84 = £20.16

Answer: The difference between the amount paid by the pupils and the total cost of the visit is £20.16.

Avoid making mistakes; read the question carefully. The entry fee is 'per person', so multiply by the number of people. The journey is two way, so double the mileage. The worksheets are only available in sets of 30, so round up.

Practice questions

41   Twenty-eight pupils each make a contribution of six pounds fifty pence towards the cost of a school trip. How much is this in total?

42   One hundred and fifty pupils in a school are supplied with a free hot meal every day. The cook works on a budget of three pounds fifty per meal. What is the cost in total per day?

43   A class did a six-mile sponsored walk for charity. In total, they raised twelve pounds forty pence per mile. How much did they raise in total?

44   The school newsletter costs three pence per page to produce. The Autumn edition consists of six pages. How much will it cost to produce two hundred copies? Give your answer in pounds.

45   A minibus travels fifty miles in one day and uses nought point three litres per mile. Fuel costs one pound thirty per litre. What is the cost of the fuel for the day?

46   The cost of a school trip is two hundred and forty pounds per pupil. Five-eighths of this is for accommodation. What is the cost of accommodation per pupil?

47   £456.42 profit has been raised from the school fete. Of this profit, $\frac{1}{3}$ was taken in the tea tent, with $\frac{5}{8}$ of this being made from the sale of cakes. How much of the total raised was made from the sale of cakes? Give your answer to the nearest penny.

48 A teacher submits a travel claim for attending external training sessions. Here is a summary of her claim.

Date	Details of claim
5 March	45 miles: school to training venue and 45 miles return
19 March	36 miles school to teachers' centre and 36 miles return
26 March	Return train fare: £45.50
	6 miles home to station and 6 miles return
	Taxi: £9.50

Car travel is paid at 45p per mile. What is the total cost of her claim?

49 A group of 30 sixth-form English students and three adults are attending a play in London. The train tickets cost £412.50 in total and the theatre tickets cost £20 for the adults. The students receive a 15% reduction on this ticket price. The total cost of the trip is to be divided evenly between everyone. How much will each person have to pay? Give your answer to the nearest whole pound.

For more examples of questions involving money calculations, see practice questions 90, 93, 99, 140, 185–187.

Conversions from one currency to another

Different countries use different currencies. In the United Kingdom, the currency is sterling (£). In France, the currency is euros (€). To convert an amount from one currency to another, you need to know the **exchange rate**.

Examples

The exchange rate is €1.6 = £1. Convert £15.50 into euros.

Answer: £15.50 = €24.80.

Write the conversion rate formula starting '£1 ='	£1 = €1.6
Write the sterling amount as a multiple of £1	£15.50 = 15.50 × £1
Substitute £1 for its equivalent	= 15.50 × €1.6
Do the calculation	= €24.80
Write the conversion rate formula starting '€1 ='	€1 = £1 ÷ 1.6
Write the euro amount as a multiple of €1	€48 = 48 × €1
Substitute €1 for its equivalent	= 48 × £1 ÷ 1.6
Do the calculation	= £48 ÷ 1.6 = £30

The exchange rate is €1.6 = £1. Convert €48 into sterling.

Answer: €48 = £30.

Practice questions

50   There are one point four euros to a pound. How many euros in spending money will a pupil get for twenty-five pounds?

51   Some sixth-form students are planning on doing voluntary work in Ghana. Each pupil requires fifteen hundred cedi, the Ghanaian currency. The exchange rate is nought point two pounds to one Ghanaian cedi. How much sponsorship money is this, in sterling, per pupil?

52   A group of art students are planning a trip to Canada to study First Nation art. They have been told they will need one hundred and fifty pounds in spending money. One point seven Canadian dollars are equivalent to one pound. How much spending money will each pupil have in Canadian dollars?

53   At the end of a school trip to Germany, there are three hundred and sixty euros left in the budget. Twenty pupils were on the trip. The money left over is to be divided equally between them. How much refund will each pupil receive in pounds sterling? The rate is one point two euros to the pound.

54   A US dollar is worth £0.63. A piece of science equipment has been ordered from the US. It costs US$567. What is the cost in pounds sterling?

55   A group of geography students are going to Iceland. The exchange rate is 1:0.0052 (krona to pounds sterling). One student plans to take £65 spending money. How many Icelandic krona will he get?

56   The exchange rate of pounds sterling to euros is 4:5. Pupils are taking £60 in spending money. One pupil spends €50 and takes the rest home again. The exchange rate on return is €15 to £13. How much money will he have when he exchanges back to pounds sterling? Give your answer to the nearest penny.

57   The cost of a school trip for 25 pupils is summarised in the table:

Accommodation (total)	€1750
Channel train	£69 per person
Entry fees to attractions	£1000
Sundries	£870
Spending money	€40 per person

What is the estimated total cost per pupil in £? Use the ratio £5 to €8.

58   For a school trip to Belgium, each pupil is allowed to take £75 spending money. The exchange rate on the way to Belgium was £1 = €1.23. One pupil spent €76 and exchanged the rest back into pounds sterling on her return. The exchange rate on return was £1 = €1.17. How much money did she exchange on the return journey? Give your answer to the nearest whole pound.

Time

There are 60 seconds in every minute, 60 minutes in every hour, 24 hours in every day and 7 days in a week. In a school, though, there are only 5 days in the week, and the important measures of time are class length and teaching day length.

Notice that questions may present time using the 12-hour clock, indicating morning with a.m. and afternoon with p.m. Alternatively, the 24-hour clock may be used, where 12:00 is noon and 24:00 is midnight.

Examples

Pupils in Year 9 are visiting a museum. The coach journey takes thirty-five minutes each way. They are spending four hours at the museum and must be back at school by three p.m. What is the latest time they must leave in the morning? Give your answer using the 24-hour clock.

Calculate the total time: 4 hours + 2 × 35 minutes = 5 hours 10 minutes

Remember to multiply the 35 minutes by 2 as it is a return journey, not one way.

Calculate the time to leave: 5 hours 10 minutes back from 15:00 is 09:50

Don't use 'normal' subtraction for time: 15:00 − 5:10 ≠ 9:90

Answer: The time to leave is 09:50.

A teacher offers after-school time slots to parents for consultations on three consecutive days. She allows 15 minutes per consultation and needs to make 28 appointments. She will start the sessions at 16:00 on the Monday and finish at 19:30 at the latest, with a break of 20 minutes at 18:00. Assuming she fills every slot consecutively, at what time will she finish on the Wednesday evening?

15 minutes per consultation: time for 4 per hour.

28 appointments: @ 4 per hour, 7 hours needed.

Session starts at 16:00 and ends at 19:30. Time available = 3.5 hours.

Don't forget to allow time for the break.

Allowing for break at 18:00: 8 consultations before the break and 4 after.

Time for 12 per evening, so 24 in two evenings, Monday and Tuesday.

Third evening: Wednesday: 4 consultations remaining. Finish time: 17:00.

Answer: The finish time is 17:00 on Wednesday.

Practice questions

59   Each school day consists of six lessons, each of fifty minutes. How many hours per day are spent in lessons?

60   A school day consists of four hours and forty minutes' lesson time per day. How much time per week is spent in lessons? Give your answer in hours and minutes.

61   Pupils have four hours and twenty minutes of mathematics per week. Two and a half hours of this is teacher-led. How many minutes per week do the pupils spend in class working independently?

62 One- third of the school day is spent in registration, tutor time and breaks. The school day is six hours and thirty minutes long. How many hours are allocated to lessons?

63 The music teacher is arranging a school concert. There are 12 planned musical items, lasting an average of 8 minutes per item. The concert starts at 19:30, with a 20-minute break in the middle. This break usually goes on for 10% longer than planned and there has to be a 3-minute break between items to allow for pupils to set up their instruments. What time should the concert finish? Give your answer in the 24-hour clock.

For more examples of questions involving time, see practice questions 104, 116, 118, 121–122, 151–152, 188–189, 209–212.

Distance

Distance is a measure of length, usually measured in millimetres (mm), centimetres (cm), metres (m) or kilometres (km).

10mm = 1cm   100cm = 1m   1000m = 1km

The **perimeter** is the distance around a shape.

Examples

An exercise book is nought point six centimetres thick. How many can be stacked on a shelf thirty-one centimetres deep?

$$\frac{31\text{cm}}{0.6\text{cm}} = 51.66 = 51$$

Although 51.66 rounds to 52 when using 'to the nearest whole number', in this circumstance, it's necessary to round down. The remaining space is not big enough for an additional book.

Answer: 51 books can be stacked.

For a charity fundraiser, pupils are asked to bring one penny coins which are laid out in a straight row. The diameter of a one penny coin is 2.1cm. Altogether 452 coins are collected. How long is the line of coins? Give your answer in metres to one decimal place.

2.1cm × 452 = 949.2cm

100cm = 1m

949.2cm = 9.5m

Answer: The line of coins is 9.5m long.

Practice questions

64 A sponsored walk is taking place around the perimeter path of the school grounds, which are rectangular. The length is six hundred metres and the width is four hundred metres. What is the total distance in kilometres?

65 A teacher travels eight point three miles each way to a technology course, held over six sessions. How many miles does she travel to and from the course in total? Give your answer to the nearest whole mile.

66 A PE teacher estimates that he runs the length of the football pitch ten times in every sports lesson. The football pitch is ninety metres long and he teaches sixteen sports lessons per week. How far does he run in one week, according to his estimate? Give your answer in kilometres to one decimal place.

67 A box file containing exam papers measures seven centimetres in depth. How many can be stacked in one pile in a wall cupboard which is one point nought three metres deep?

68 A sponsored walk takes place around the school grounds, with each lap an estimated 1700m in length. The results are recorded:

Number of laps	Number of pupils
3	3
4	4
5	18
6	13

What is the total distance in kilometres walked by all the pupils? Give your answer to one decimal place.

69 A Duke of Edinburgh hike is divided into the following sections: $\frac{1}{3}$ flat ground; $\frac{1}{8}$ through forest; $\frac{2}{5}$ uphill; the rest is mixed terrain. The total hike is 18 miles. What is the distance over mixed terrain? Give your answer to one decimal place.

70 A geography class uses maps with a scale of 1:100,000. Pupils are estimating the length of a river from source to estuary by dividing it into sections on the map and measuring each section.

The distance of each section is recorded in centimetres: 1.4; 5.6; 3.9; 7.4; 2.2.

What is the estimated length of the river in kilometres based on these measurements?

For more examples of questions involving distance, see practice questions 85, 87–88, 90–92, 103, 106, 185–187, 209–212.

Area

Area is a two-dimensional measure and is calculated by multiplying two lengths: the length and width of an object, or its height and width. Area is usually measured in square millimetres (mm^2), square centimetres (cm^2), square metres (m^2) or square kilometres (km^2).

Examples

A new flowerbed is planned for the school grounds. It will measure three point two metres by one point five metres. What is its area? Give your answer in square metres.

$3.2\text{m} \times 1.5\text{m} = 4.8\text{m}^2$

Answer: The area is 4.8m^2.

A sheet of A4 paper is two hundred and ten millimetres long and two hundred and ninety-seven millimetres wide. What is its area? Give your answer in square centimetres.

Area = length × width = 210mm × 297mm = 62,370mm² = 623.7cm²

 1cm = 10mm but 1cm² ≠ 100mm². 1cm² = 10mm × 10mm = 100mm².

Convert the lengths to the units needed in the answer before doing the calculation.

Answer: The area is 623.7cm^2.

Questions on area can require other skills, like fractions.

A small fish pond is to be made in the school grounds. Its area is planned to be one point five metres by one point two metres in an area of grass measuring nine square metres. What fraction of the area of grass is allocated to the fish pond?

Area = $1.5\text{m} \times 1.2\text{m} = 1.8\text{m}^2$

1.8m^2 out of $9\text{m}^2 = 1.8 \div 9 = \dfrac{18}{90} = \dfrac{1}{5}$

Answer: $\dfrac{1}{5}$ is allocated to the fish pond.

Practice questions

71 The art department has a display board measuring six hundred centimetres by four hundred centimetres. What is the area in square metres?

72 The area of the school hockey pitch is four thousand eight hundred and sixty square metres and the length is ninety metres. What is the width?

73 The school football pitch is one hundred and twenty metres long and its area is six thousand square metres. What is the width of the football pitch?

74 Below is a cross section of the school swimming pool.
At the shallow end, the depth is 1m and at the deep end the depth is 2m. The length of the pool is 25m.

Calculate the area of the cross section. Give your answer in m².

75 A new classroom is to be built for the art department, 9m wide and 10m long. Windows, doors and cupboards will take up the equivalent of 9m in length. Exhibition spaces are planned for as much of the space as possible, although the maximum usable height above the floor for displays is 2m and the minimum height is 0.5m. How much area can be devoted to exhibition space?

76 A primary school science lesson is looking at the number of daisies per square metre on the school lawn. They divide the lawn into 15 equally sized rectangles for counting purposes. The lawn measures 6 metres by 10 metres. What is the area of one small rectangle for counting purposes?

77 In a mathematics lesson, Year 4 pupils are looking at the area of the school playground. They use a measuring wheel to estimate the dimensions and draw a diagram of their findings.

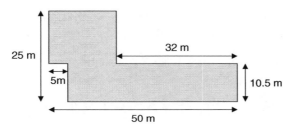

Calculate the total area of the playground.

Volume and capacity

Volume is a three-dimensional measure and is calculated by multiplying three lengths: the height, length and width of an object. Volume is usually measured in cubic millimetres (mm^3), cubic centimetres (cm^3), cubic metres (m^3) or cubic kilometres (km^3).

Capacity is a measure of how much can fill a volume of space. Capacity is usually measured in millilitres (ml), centilitres (cl) or litres (l).

1 litre occupies $1000cm^3$ of space.

Examples

In a mathematics lesson, pupils are making cubes out of cardboard. The length of one side must be five centimetres. What is the volume of the cube?

   $5cm \times 5cm \times 5cm = 125cm^3$

Answer: The volume is $125cm^3$.

A packing chest is thirty centimetres by thirty centimetres by fifty centimetres. What is its volume? Give your answer in cubic metres.

   Volume = $30cm \times 30cm \times 50cm = 4500cm^3 = 4500/1,000,000m^3 = 0.0045m^3$

Convert the lengths to the units needed in the answer before doing the calculation.

$1m = 100cm$ but $1m^3 \neq 100cm^3$. $1m^3 = 100cm \times 100cm \times 100cm = 1,000,000cm^3$

Answer: The volume is $0.0045m^3$.

Practice questions

78   What is the height of a classroom which has a volume of two hundred and twenty-four cubic metres, length eight metres and width seven metres?

79   To prepare for some chemistry experiments, the teacher needs to divide three litres of liquid equally between seventy-five bottles. How much will be poured into each bottle? Give your answer in millilitres.

80   A primary school teacher planned to keep goldfish in the classroom. How many litres are needed to fill a small fish tank measuring fifty centimetres by thirty centimetres by twenty centimetres? Assume the tank will be filled to the top.

81   A science experiment requires dilution of acid to water in the ratio of 2:50. The teacher uses half a litre of water. How much acid should be used? Give your answer in cm^3.

82   A small storage box measures $12'' \times 12'' \times 15''$. What is the volume in cm^3? Use the conversion rate of 2.5cm to 1″.

Conversions from one measure to another

Different countries use different units of measure. In England, distances are measured in miles. In France, kilometres (km) are used.

To convert a distance from one measure to another, you need to know the conversion formula. This is usually given as an equation.

Examples

Taking 5 miles to be equivalent to 8 kilometres, convert 12km into miles.

Write the conversion rate formula starting '1km ='	$1km = \dfrac{5}{8}$ miles
Write the kilometre distance as a multiple of 1km	$12km = 12 \times 1km$
Substitute 1km for its equivalent in miles	$= 12 \times \dfrac{5}{8}$ miles
Do the calculation	$= 7.5$ miles

Answer: 12km = 7.5 miles.

Taking 5 miles to be equivalent to 8 kilometres, convert 35 miles into kilometres.

Write the conversion rate formula starting '1 mile ='	$1 \text{ mile} = \dfrac{8}{5}$ km
Write the distance as a multiple of 1 mile	$35 \text{ miles} = 35 \times 1 \text{ mile}$
Substitute 1 mile for its equivalent in kilometres	$= 35 \times \dfrac{8}{5}$ km
Do the calculation	$= 56km$

Answer: 35 miles = 56km.

Practice questions

83   Pupils travelling to France are calculating the total distance they will travel. From the French ferry port to their hotel is a distance of thirty-two kilometres. Use the approximation of five miles to eight kilometres. Calculate how many miles they will travel from the port to the hotel.

84   A technology teacher wants to use an old cake recipe with his class. The recipe requires eight ounces of flour. How many grams is this? Use the conversion of one ounce equals twenty-eight point four grams. Give your answer to the nearest gram.

85   Students are researching heights of their ancestors. One grandmother states she is five feet in height. What is this in metres? Use the conversion of thirty centimetres to one foot.

86   What is fifty-nine degrees Fahrenheit in degrees centigrade? To convert from Fahrenheit to centigrade, subtract thirty-two, then multiply by five and divide by nine.

87   This is a summary of the distances the school minibus will cover on a trip to France:

Distance from the school to the ferry port:	165 miles
Distance from ferry port in France to hotel:	144km
Estimated distance covered during the stay in France	192km
Odometer reading at the start (in miles)	50,132

What will the odometer read at the end of the trip? Use the ratio of 5 miles to 8 kilometres.

88   A school trip is planned for France. From the ferry port to the hotel is a distance of 279km one way. While staying in France, it is estimated that a further 186km will be travelled. From the school to the ferry is a distance of 55 miles. What is the ratio of the distance travelled in the UK to the distance travelled in France? Use the conversion rate of 5 miles to 8km.

89   To convert °F to °C, the pupils in a science lesson used the following method:

'Subtract 32, multiply by 5 and divide by 9'.

The pupils take two readings at set times of a liquid as it cools down. The first reading is 194°F and the second is 95°F. By how many °C has the liquid cooled?

90   A geography teacher is planning a short trip to the Lake District, using the school minibus.

The total distance of the trip is estimated to be 455 miles.

The fuel consumption of the minibus is estimated to be 35 miles per gallon.

Fuel costs £1.32 per litre.

Use the conversion of 1 gallon to 4.55 litres. What is the estimated cost of the fuel for the weekend? Give your answer to the nearest whole pound.

91   A teacher is going on a conference 45 miles away. His car does an average of 40 miles to the gallon (mpg). Use the conversion rate of 1 litre equivalent to 0.2 gallons.

How many litres of fuel will he need to travel to and from the conference? Give your answer to two decimal places.

For more examples of questions involving converting between different measures, see practice questions 211–212.

3.3   Statistics

When surveys are carried out and lots of data is collected, the challenge is to understand what the data can tell you. Statistics derived from the data help, allowing comparisons to be made.

Averages

An **average** is a single value chosen or calculated to represent a group of values. There are three different averages – mean, mode and median – each useful in its own way, depending on the range and spread of the data it is representing.

Mean

The **mean** is calculated by adding up all the values and then dividing by the number of values. The mean value might not coincide with an actual data value. It represents a balance point in that there is as much above it as below. For data that is 'normal' with an even **distribution**, the mean is a useful measure but can be skewed by very low or very high results.

Example

A team of four children were selected for a relay race. Their best times in seconds were eighty-three point four, seventy-nine point eight, ninety-one point three and seventy-six point five. What is their mean running time in seconds? Give your answer to one decimal place.

Add up all the data items	$83.4 + 79.8 + 91.3 + 76.5 = 331$
Divide by the number of data items	$331 \div 4 = 82.75$
Give the answer to the required accuracy	$82.75 = 82.8$ (to 1 dp)

Do not round the data before working out the mean.

Answer: The mean running time is 82.8 seconds (to 1 dp).

Practice questions

92   A class carried out a survey to find out how far people lived from the school. In total, the twenty-five pupils lived sixty-five kilometres from the school. What is the mean distance travelled? Give your answer in metres.

93   A test has a maximum total of sixty marks. Pupil A scores twenty-four and pupil B scores thirty-six. What is their mean score as a percentage?

94   The table overleaf shows a set of test results (in %) achieved by one class.

34	46	67	76	23	98	67
56	57	66	34	67	39	89
45	67	99	67	43	56	77

What is the mean mark gained? Give your answer to the nearest whole number.

95 Six pupils in Year 7 are selected at random to take an additional reading test. Their actual ages to the nearest month are: 11 years 6 months; 11 years 9 months; 11 years 11 months; 11 years 2 months; 11 years 10 months; 11 years 4 months.

What is the mean age in years and months?

96 Pupils are studying weather patterns and record the midday temperature in °C over a period of five weeks in the winter.

	Mon	Tue	Wed	Thu	Fri
Week 1	−1	0	1	2	4
Week 2	3	2	−4	−3	−2
Week 3	2	2	1	0	0
Week 4	−3	−1	1	2	3
Week 5	4	0	0	−1	−4

What is the mean temperature in week 4? Give your answer to one decimal place.

97 A pupil obtained the following marks in four tests:

Test A: 13/20; Test B: 16/25; Test C: 22/40; Test D: 19/30.

What is her average mark as a decimal? Give your answer to two decimal places.

98 Ninety pupils take part in a sponsored walk and raise £832.50 in total. What is the mean average amount raised per pupil?

99 This term, 25 pupils took part in a sponsored swim. The teacher recorded the number of lengths each pupil completed.

Number of lengths	Number of pupils
10	5
11	6
12	7
13	4
14	3

The mean sponsorship per length was £3.25. How much money was raised in total?

100 Last week, 32 pupils took a test. Their mean score was 54%. One pupil was absent and took the test on his return. He scored 21%. What is the revised mean for the group?

Age – for actual age and reading age – is measured in years and months. This may be written as year. month (where the dot is not a decimal point!) or year-month.

For more examples of questions involving calculating a mean, see practice questions 113–116, 118– 119, 122, 124–125, 130, 141, 145, 162, 166, 172–173, 177, 209.

Median

The **median** is the middlemost value when the values are arranged in order. If there is an even number of values, the mean of the middlemost two values is calculated as the median value. For large amounts of data, the data may be tallied, or grouped. The median can also be read from a **cumulative frequency** graph (see page 81 for an example of this type of graph) and may also be displayed on a **box and whisker** plot (page 82).

Example

A Year 7 science group is studying plant growth under different conditions. The table below records 50 plants grown in a heated environment.

Height	Frequency
0 < h ≤ 6	10
6 < h ≤ 8	16
8 < h ≤ 10	11
10 < h ≤ 12	7
12 < h ≤ 14	4
14 < h ≤ 16	1
16 < h ≤ 20	1

Don't look at the middle category. Imagine all the samples lined up in a row in order of size.

What is the median height category?

There are 50 data items (heights of plants) so the median is the average of the 25th and 26th items. To identify these data items, extend the table to include the cumulative frequency and look where the 25th and 26th items lie.

Height	Frequency	Cumulative frequency
0 < h ≤ 6	10	10
6 < h ≤ 8	**16**	**26**
8 < h ≤ 10	11	37
10 < h ≤ 12	7	44

Height	Frequency	Cumulative frequency
12 < h ≤ 14	4	48
14 < h ≤ 16	1	49
16 < h ≤ 20	1	50

Check that the top value in the cumulative frequency column agrees with the total number of plants as given in the stem of the question.

Answer: The median height category is $6 < h \leq 8$.

The median is the middlemost value, not the middle of the range.

Practice questions

101   25 pupils take part in a sponsored swim. The teacher records the number of lengths each pupil completes. What is the median number of lengths?

Number of lengths	Number of pupils
10				
11	卌|
12					
13	卌| ||||
14	卌		

If the frequency reaches 5, the four tally marks are 'crossed' with the fifth to make a 'gate' 卌.

102   A survey of 100 pupils was carried out to determine how many siblings each had. The results were summarised:

Number of siblings	0	1	2	3	4	5
Number of children	24	42	17	9	6	2

What is the median number of siblings per child?

103   A sponsored walk takes place around the school grounds, with each lap an estimated 1700m in length. The results are recorded:

Number of laps	Number of pupils
2	3
3	3
4	4
5	11
6	20

What is the median distance in kilometres walked by the pupils?

For more examples of questions involving identifying a median, see practice questions 105, 111, 114–116, 118, 140, 145, 160, 162, 164, 167, 175, 190, 197–198, 200.

Mode

The mode is the value that occurs most frequently. It is the data value with the highest frequency. If you are presented with a lot of data, you might first need to tally the data and produce a summary of it. Because the mode provides the 'most popular' data value, it is useful to know if trying to meet the needs of as many as possible, eg in supplying uniforms to fit the majority.

Example

A survey is carried out on pupils' shoe sizes. What is the modal shoe size?

5	6	3	8	4
7	6	10	7	8
9	5	9	9	4

To identify the mode, identify the smallest and largest shoe sizes (3 and 10) and create a tally chart, making one mark for every time that shoe size appears in the data.

Size	3	4	5	6	7	8	9	10
Frequency																	

Answer: Size 9 is the modal shoe size.

Practice questions

104 A group of 14 pupils are timed completing a problem-solving task. The results, to the nearest whole second, are as follows:

12   15   27   14   19   22   27   13   27   22   18   22   16   22

What is the modal number of seconds taken to complete the test?

105 This term, 25 pupils took part in a sponsored swim. The teacher recorded the number of lengths each pupil completed.

Number of lengths	Number of pupils
10	Ⅼⅼⅼⅼ
11	Ⅼⅼⅼⅼ Ⅰ
12	Ⅼⅼⅼⅼ ⅠⅠ
13	ⅠⅠⅠⅠ
14	ⅠⅠⅠ

What was the modal number of lengths?

106 A sponsored walk takes place around the school grounds, with each lap an estimated 1700m in length. The results are recorded:

Number of laps	Number of pupils
2	3
3	3
4	4
5	11
6	20

What is the modal distance in kilometres walked by the pupils?

For more examples of questions involving identifying a mode, see practice questions 104, 106, 115, 118–119, 164, 173.

Range

The range is the difference between the highest and lowest values and gives a measure of the **spread** of the data.

Example

A survey is carried out on pupils' shoe sizes. What is the range of shoe sizes?

5	6	3	8	4
7	6	10	7	8
9	5	9	9	4

To identify the range, identify the smallest and largest shoe sizes (3 and 10) and calculate the difference:

10 − 3 = 7

Answer: The range of shoe sizes is 7.

Practice questions

107 These are the test results achieved by one class.

34	46	67	76	23	98	67
56	57	66	34	67	39	89
45	67	99	67	43	56	77

What is the range of the marks gained?

A comparison was made between five schools' GCSE results. The table shows the percentage of pupils out of the total number gaining A*/A–C grades, rounded to one decimal place.

School	2012	2013	2014
A*/A	62.5	61.9	59.6
B	72.8	75.4	76.9
C	45.6	48.9	50.2
D	59.6	58.4	57.9
E	86.3	85.4	79.1

108 What is the range in 2012?

109 What is the difference between the range in year 2013 and in year 2014?

110 The reading ages of a group of Year 6 pupils receiving additional help was assessed.

Pupil	Actual age		Reading age	
	Years	Months	Years	Months
1	11	0	10	9
2	10	6	10	5
3	10	8	8	3
4	10	4	9	1
5	10	11	9	11
6	10	7	10	7

What is the difference between the ranges of actual age and reading age? Give your answer in months.

For more examples of questions involving calculating a range, see practice questions 112, 115, 117, 119, 164, 173, 192–196, 199–200.

Interquartile range

While the range is an indication of the spread of all the data, the interquartile range is an indication of where the middle half of the data lies.

In the same way that the median identifies the middlemost value, when the data is arranged in order, the **lower quartile** is the middlemost value of the bottom half, and the **upper quartile** is the middlemost value of the upper half.

The quartiles cut the data into quarters, and the middle two quartiles show the interquartile range.

Practice questions involving quartiles and interquartile ranges appear later as they usually relate to a box and whisker plot (page 82) or a cumulative frequency curve (page 81).

Combinations of measures of average

In the test, you are not required to decide on which average to use. You will however be required to interpret the data through different averages.

Refer to the 'Areas of numeracy' support materials available on the DfE website, for more detailed descriptions of mean, mode and median to help you to understand under what conditions each might be used.

Several questions may be set for a single set of data.

Practice questions

Pupils are studying weather patterns and record the midday temperature in °C over a period of five weeks in the winter.

	Mon	Tue	Wed	Thu	Fri
Week 1	−1	0	1	2	4
Week 2	3	2	−4	−3	−2
Week 3	2	2	1	0	0
Week 4	−3	−1	1	2	3
Week 5	4	0	0	−1	−4

111 What is the median temperature in week 2?

112 What is the range of the temperatures recorded?

113 Point and click on the week that has the highest mean temperature.

Make sure you know which average you need to give: the mean, the median or the mode.

A single question may require you to calculate more than one type of average, or the range.

Practice questions

114 A comparison was made between five schools' GCSE results. The table shows the percentage of pupils out of the total number gaining five A*/A–C grades, rounded to one decimal place.

School	2012	2013	2014
A*/A	62.5	61.9	59.6
B	72.8	75.4	76.9
C	45.6	48.9	50.2
D	59.6	58.4	57.9
E	86.3	85.4	79.1

What is the difference between the mean percentage and the median percentage in 2013?

115 Pupils are studying weather patterns and record the midday temperature in °C over a period of three weeks in the winter.

	Mon	Tue	Wed	Thu	Fri
Week 1	−4	−3	−1	0	0
Week 2	4	2	−1	−3	−2
Week 3	0	2	2	4	5

Select all the true statements:

A. The median temperature is higher than the mean temperature in week 1.

B. The range of temperatures is 5°C.

C. The data is bimodal.

D. The mean temperature in week 2 is 0°C.

116 The running times for six pupils were recorded during athletics practice.

Pupil	Time in secs
A	94.2
B	86.1
C	92.5
D	110.4
E	108.3
F	97.1

What is the difference between the mean and the median running times?

117 Test results for two groups have been summarised in the table. The maximum possible mark for the test was 100.

Class	Lowest test score	Median	Highest test score
Set 2	11	42	93
Set 4	15	51	85

Select the true statement(s):

A. Set 2 did better at the test than Set 4.

B. The range of marks was greater for Set 2 than for Set 4.

C. At least half of all the pupils taking the test scored 43 or more.

118 The following table shows the time taken by eight Year 6 pupils to complete an obstacle course.

Pupil	Time taken (secs)
1	85.0
2	78.7
3	75.1
4	66.3
5	87.5
6	92.2
7	102.0
8	101.2

Select all the true statements:

A. There is no mode.

B. The mean time taken is 1 minute 43 secs.

C. The median time is 85.0 secs.

D. Pupil 4's was the fastest time by 9 seconds to the nearest second.

119 A class teacher is looking at the attendance of his class over a six-week period. There are 28 children in the class.

	Mon	Tue	Wed	Thu	Fri
Week 1	28	26	27	27	25
Week 2	25	26	23	22	24
Week 3	28	28	27	26	21
Week 4	22	24	25	25	26
Week 5	28	23	22	24	20

Select all the true statements:

A. The mean attendance on Mondays is three higher than the mean attendance on Fridays.

B. The range of attendance is 7.

C. The modal attendance in week 1 is 27.

3.4   Presentation of data

 Raw data presented simply as a list of numbers in the order in which it is collected can be difficult to interpret. When converted to a tabulated format, or presented in diagrammatic form, this shows 'at a glance' various aspects of the data:

○ Most/least popular is given by

   the largest/smallest share of a pie chart

   the longest/shortest bars in a bar chart

   the highest/lowest points on a line graph.

○ The range or spread of the data is given by

   the axis labelling on a bar chart or graph

   the whiskers on a boxplot.

○ Totals can be calculated

   by adding all the numbers in one row, or in one column

   by reading values from a cumulative frequency curve.

Tables

Presenting data in tables not only requires an understanding of how to extract relevant data from the table but also allows other aspects of numeracy to be tested. You may also be asked to complete a table by filling in the missing entries.

 At the simplest level, a question may require the summing of the values in a given row or column. If the data is presented such that a cross-casting sum can be used to check the total, use this as a method of ensuring accuracy. Otherwise, double-check every stage of the working.

Simple tables

A table sets out data in a columnar format. The column headings indicate what data has been collected and collated. The row headings show what grouping, if any, has been done.

❌ Much information is provided within the table format. It's easy to misread this information, focusing on the wrong column(s) or the wrong row(s).

Example

During a flu epidemic, the following table was compiled for a high school.

Year group	Number on roll	Proportion of pupils absent
7	205	0.20
8	210	0.10
9	188	0.25
10	185	0.20
11	180	0.30
6th form	140	0.15

How many pupils were absent?

Total absent: $(205 \times 0.2) + (210 \times 0.1) + (188 \times 0.25) + (185 \times 0.2) + (180 \times 0.3) + (140 \times 0.15)$

$= 41 + 21 + 47 + 37 + 54 + 21$

$= 221$

When there are so many calculations and it's essential that you arrive at the correct answer, double-check each step of your working.

Answer: 221 pupils were absent.

Practice questions

120 Pupils are studying weather patterns and record the midday temperature in °C over a period of five weeks in the winter.

	Mon	Tue	Wed	Thu	Fri
Week 1	3	2	−4	−3	−2
Week 2	2	2	1	0	0
Week 3	−1	0	1	2	4
Week 4	−3	−1	1	1	3
Week 5	4	0	0	−1	−4

Point and click on the week in which the temperatures steadily rose.

121 A primary school timetable is broken down into the following proportions on a Monday (see overleaf):

Subject	Proportion of the school day
English	0.25
Mathematics	0.25
Science	0.10
PE	0.15
Other	0.25

Lessons last for 5 hours per day. How much time is spent per day doing PE on Mondays? Give your answer in minutes.

 122 The running times for five pupils were recorded during athletics practice.

Pupil	Time in secs
A	94.2
B	86.1
C	92.5
D	110.4
E	108.3

What proportion of children was below the mean running time for this group? Give your answer as a decimal.

123 The following table gives the predicted and actual proportions of pupils gaining each level in Key Stage 2.

Level	2	3	4	5
Predicted	0.10	0.20	0.44	0.25
Actual	0.07	0.10	0.62	0.21

What was the proportional increase from the predicted to actual grades in level 4? Give your answer as a fraction in its lowest terms.

124 A comparison was made between five schools' GCSE results. The table shows the percentage of pupils out of the total number gaining A*/A–C grades, rounded to one decimal place.

School	2012	2013	2014
A*/A	62.5	61.9	59.6
B	72.8	75.4	76.9
C	45.6	48.9	50.2
D	59.6	58.4	57.9
E	86.3	85.4	79.1

What is the difference between the mean in 2012 and the mean in 2014? Give your answer to one decimal place.

125 A food technology group is comparing different pastry recipes.

Proportion	Recipe 1	Recipe 2	Recipe 3	Recipe 4
Flour	0.5	0.7	0.35	0.75
Fat	0.5	0.3	0.65	0.25

What is the mean amount of fat needed for the four recipes? Give your answer as a fraction in its lowest terms.

126 In a portfolio-based qualification, there are three grades: distinction, merit and pass. This table shows the results for classes 1, 2 and 3.

Class	Number of portfolios		
	Pass	Merit	Distinction
1	15	9	4
2	12	16	8
3	11	6	9

For the purposes of internal moderation, the school has a policy of selecting $\frac{1}{6}$ of each category to the nearest next whole number above. For example, if there are 9 in a category, the moderator will select 2.

How many portfolios will be selected in total?

Completion of missing entries

The next set of questions requires the completion of missing entries in tables.

Practice questions

127 A learning support assistant used some new resources with a small group of pupils in a mathematics class. She tested the pupils before and after they used the new resources and analysed the results.

Pupil	Test results (%)		% difference
	Before	After	
A	55	74	+19
B	42	48	+6
C	39	35	
D	22	23	
E	44	56	

Select and place the % differences into the correct cells.

| −12 | −4 | −1 | 0 | +1 | +4 | +8 | +10 | +12 |

128 A school's prediction for Key Stage 2 results is shown in the table.

	Number of pupils predicted for each grade		
Level	English	Mathematics	Science
2	2	4	6
3	9	11	
4	28	25	20
5	7	6	8

Complete the table and then calculate the proportion of the year group that is predicted to gain below a level 5 in science. Give your answer as a fraction in its lowest terms.

129 The table shows the achievement of pupils at Key Stage 2 over a three-year period.

Year	Level 3	Level 4	Level 5
2012	6	8	4
% of total	33	44	23
2013	6	12	6
% of total	25	50	25
2014	7		9
% of total	22	50	28

Select from the numbers below to insert in the correct boxes.

| 6 | 12 | 16 | 22 | 23 | 25 | 50 | 75 |

130 Reading ages were compared between boys and girls in Years 4, 5 and 6.

	Mean reading age (years-months)		
	Year 4	Year 5	Year 6
Boys	8-1	9-0	10-2
Girls	8-7	9-5	10-5

What is the mean difference in reading ages (to the nearest whole number) between boys and girls for Years 4, 5 and 6?

Drag and drop the correct values to complete the table:

2	3	4	5	6

Difference between boys' and girls' mean reading ages (months)			Mean difference for Years 4, 5 and 6
Year 4	Year 5	Year 6	
	5		

Multiple questions set against one table

More than one question could be set from a single table of data.

Read the question carefully to establish which row/column of which table holds the data to be used to work out the answer.

Practice questions

A table has been produced to show which pupils in a primary school live in the village in which the school is situated.

Class	Number of pupils	Number of pupils living in the village
R	16	7
1	18	10
2	22	12
3	17	13
4	19	11
5	25	18
6	19	14

131 What percentage of pupils in the school live in the village in which the school is situated? Give your answer to the nearest whole number.

132 Taking each individual year group, calculate the largest proportion of pupils living in the village in which the school is situated. Give your answer as a percentage to one decimal place.

The table shows the achievement of pupils at Key Stage 2 over a three-year period.

Year	Level 3	Level 4	Level 5
2012	6	8	4
2013	6	12	6
2014	3	15	6

133 In which year did the smallest proportion of pupils gain level 5?

134 What percentage of pupils gained level 4 in year 2012? Answer to the nearest whole number.

8	23	42	44	47	50	63

The Key Stage 2 levels of Year 6 pupils in a large primary school were analysed by the class.

Level	Class 6 (1)	Class 6 (2)	Class 6 (3)
2	2	4	0
3	7	7	6
4	12	13	16
5	8	2	4
6	0	0	1

135 What percentage of the total year group achieved level 4 and above, to the nearest whole number?

56	68	69	76	82	86	93

136 Point and click on the class which achieved the highest percentage of level 3 grades at Key Stage 2.

A school analyses its GCSE results in the core subjects of English, mathematics, science and a humanities subject. The results are summarised in the table below. All percentages are rounded to the nearest whole number.

Grade	Number of pupils			
	English	Mathematics	Science	Humanities
A*–A	45	42	52	57
B–C	88	79	67	
D–E	56		52	46
F–G	22	41	40	34
	211	211	211	211
	English	Mathematics	Science	Humanities
% A*–C	63		56	27
% A*–E		81		84
% A*–G	100	100	100	100

137 Drag and drop the correct values to complete the table.

37	43	44	49	5	57	64	74	81	90

138 The English department has set a target of increasing the number of A*–C grades by six percentage points for the following academic year. Assuming there will be the same number of pupils taking GCSEs, how many more pupils will need to achieve grades A*–C?

Multiple tables

More than one table may be provided!

Practice questions

139 A group of pupils was tested for their reading age on two different occasions.

Autumn term			Summer term		
Pupil	Actual age years-months	Reading age years-months	Pupil	Actual age years-months	Reading age years-months
A	8-11	7-5	A	9-5	7-9
B	8-4	8-4	B	8-10	9-0
C	8-6	8-8	C	9-0	9-2
D	8-7	8-9	D	9-1	9-9
E	9-1	9-3	E	9-7	10-3
F	8-3	8-11	F	8-9	9-7
G	8-1	8-0	G	8-7	8-7
H	8-4	9-3	H	8-10	9-9

Click on the letters for pupils who showed an improvement of more than 4 months in the difference between the actual age and the reading age between the autumn and the summer terms.

140 At the end of the summer term, a school has a fund-raising week. Pupils choose to do different activities for charity. The tables summarise three of the fund-raising events. The money raised is to be divided between charity A and charity B in the ratio of 3:2.

Sponsored activities		School fete		Sales in school	
Activity	Amount raised	Item	Amount raised	Type	Amount raised
Swimming	£89.45	Refreshments	£167.22	Magazines	£67.50
Walking	£93.87	Tombola	£75.50	Cakes	£35.20
Running	£145.35	Stalls	£105.43	Crafts	£68.30

Select all the true statements:

A. Of the activities listed, the highest total amount of money raised was at the school fete.

B. Charity A will receive £509 to the nearest whole £.

C. The median amount raised of all the items listed is £89.45.

More than one question could be set from such tables of data. Note that question 143 also requires completion of entries.

Practice questions

From 2011 to 2014, a primary school's pupils' performance in reading in Key Stage 1 was tested and compared with the national averages.

Year	Percentage of boys at level 2 and above (school)	Percentage of boys at level 2 and above (national average)	Percentage of girls at level 2 and above (school)	Percentage of girls at level 2 and above (national average)
2011	76.4	75.3	86.3	85.9
2012	79.6	78.7	87.4	86.2
2013	75.8	78.3	88.1	87.5
2014	78.5	78.7	89.2	87.4
2015				

Source: www.gov.uk/government/collections/statistics-key-stage-2

 141 What is the difference between the mean average over the four-year period 2011–2014, between the boys' performance in the school and the national average for the boys? Give your answer to one decimal place.

142 Select the correct statements:

A. The performance of the boys in the school is consistently below the national average.

B. The percentage of girls in the school achieving level 2 and above has increased every year.

C. The girls in the school consistently outperform the boys.

D. In 2013, the boys in the school were performing at 2.5% below the national average for that year.

143 The school predicts that the percentage of pupils in the school achieving level 2 and above will increase in 2015 by 0.6% for both boys and girls. The national averages are expected to rise by 0.2%.

Drag and drop the correct amounts into the table:

| 75.5 | 77.0 | 78.7 | 78.9 | 79.1 | 79.3 | 86.1 | 86.9 | 87.6 | 88.0 | 89.4 | 89.8 | 91.5 |

Ten pupils in a Year 5 group were given additional mathematics support in an attempt to raise their achievement. They were given a task before and after the additional support. The task was marked out of 40 and the results analysed according to gender.

Pupil	Girls' task score before additional support	Girls' task score after additional support
A	15	22
B	20	25
C	32	34
D	16	19
E	25	21

Pupil	Boys' task score before additional support	Boys' task score after additional support
F	20	32
G	16	19
H	17	28
I	29	33
J	31	38

144 Point and click on the pupil who made the most improvement after the additional support.

145 Indicate the true statement(s):

   A. All the boys achieved improved scores after the additional support.

   B. 20% of the girls achieved a lower score after the additional support.

   C. The mean difference in the boys' scores before and after the additional support was 7.4.

   D. The median girls' score after the additional support was 25 marks.

   E. Pupil G scored 47.5% in the task after additional support.

Two-way tables

Two-way tables allow comparison of different sets of tables.

Totals are usually shown on the opposite side of the table from the category heading.

Be sure to read the correct row and column from the correct table!

Practice questions

146 A student teacher is researching into a possible link between ability in mathematics and in music. She presents the GCSE results of a group of pupils in a two-way table.

		GCSE music			
GCSE mathematics	GCSE grade	A*–A	B–C	D–E	F–G
	A*–A	5	6	2	0
	B–C	4	7	3	1
	D–E	3	4	5	2
	F–G	0	1	1	7

Indicate all the true statements:

A. Approximately $\frac{1}{10}$ of the pupils who took GCSE mathematics and GCSE music gained grades A* or A in both subjects.

B. More than $\frac{1}{6}$ of the pupils taking both GCSE mathematics and GCSE music gained grades F or G in mathematics.

C. $\frac{3}{4}$ of the pupils who gained C and above in mathematics gained A or A* in music.

More than one two-way table might be given and more than one question may be set for them.

Practice questions

A comparison is made between pupils' GCSE results in mathematics and their results in French and in music. This comparison is summarised in the two-way tables below and at the top of page 61.

		GCSE French				
GCSE mathematics	GCSE grade	A*–A	B–C	D–E	F–G	Total
	A*–A	5	8	1	–	14
	B–C	2	11	5	–	18
	D–E	3	9	11	12	35
	F–G	1	1	2	14	18
	Total	11	29	19	26	

		GCSE music				
GCSE mathematics	GCSE grade	A*–A	B–C	D–E	F–G	Total
	A*–A	3	2	2	–	7
	B–C	1	9	5	–	15
	D–E	–	3	2	2	7
	F–G	–	1	1	–	2
	Total	4	15	10	2	

147 What fraction of pupils taking both mathematics and French GCSEs gained E and above in both subjects? Give your answer as a fraction in its lowest terms.

148 The proportion of pupils achieving C and above in both GCSE music and in GCSE mathematics as a decimal to one decimal place is:

| 0.3 | | 0.31 | | 0.4 | | 0.48 | | 0.5 |

Charts

Data can be presented in chart form for a quick appreciation of proportion, as in shares of a pie chart, or for comparison, one against another, as in a bar chart.

Pie charts

In a pie chart, each sector of the circle represents a share of the total **population**.

The shares of the 'pie' can show actual values (as in practice questions 149, 150) or the percentages (as in practice questions 151, 152).

Multiple pie charts provide an easy way to compare two sets of data, eg from two different classes, different schools, different years: see for example practice questions 153–157.

Practice questions

The pastoral team at one high school is concerned about the eating habits of Years 7 and 8. A pie chart is created to look at lunchtime arrangements made by Year 7 and 8 pupils.

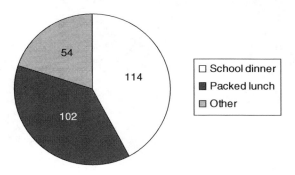

149 Select all the true statements:

A. More than 40% of pupils in Years 7 and 8 have school dinners.

B. One-fifth of the pupils make other arrangements.

C. Less than 1 in 3 pupils has a packed lunch.

150 The school puts in place a strategy to encourage more pupils to have school dinners. The following term, 24 more pupils had school dinners. What percentage of pupils now has school dinners (to the nearest whole number)?

24	29	47	51	54	126	138

The ICT teacher investigated how long the 74 pupils in the computer club spent playing computer games at home. She produced the pie chart below.

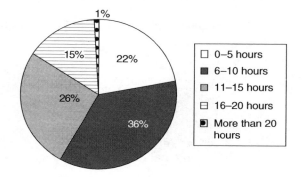

151 How many pupils spent more than 20 hours playing computer games?

152 Three more pupils join the computer club. They each played computer games for between 11 and 15 hours per week.

Point and click on the pie chart below which represents the new data.

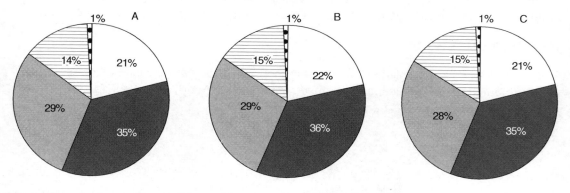

 When a question asks 'how many pupils', consider whether you should round up to the nearest whole number.

153 A group of pupils was surveyed in Year 7 and again in Year 10 to see which school clubs they attended. The results are shown in the pie charts below.

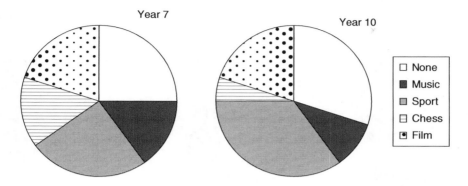

The number going to film club remains the same. Drag and drop the correct percentage values into the table below:

| 10 | 15 | 20 | 20 | 25 | 25 | 30 | 90 |

	None	**Music**	**Sport**	**Chess**	**Film**
% Year 7		15	25		
% Year 10	30	10	35	5	

The same pair of pie charts could be used for more than one question:

Practice questions

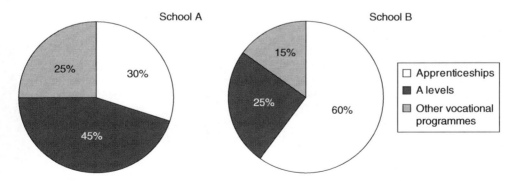

Two local high schools compare the chosen study programmes of pupils at the end of Year 11. The pie charts show the percentage of pupils taking each option.

154 School A has 103 pupils in Year 11. School B has 95 pupils in Year 11. How many pupils in total from the two schools are intending to do A levels?

155 Select all the true statement(s):

    A. A greater proportion of pupils are taking A levels at school B than at school A.

    B. One-quarter of the pupils at school A are planning on taking other vocational programmes.

    C. More than half the pupils at school B are planning on doing an apprenticeship.

The head of the mathematics department compares GCSE results for Year 11 over a two-year period and produces pie charts:

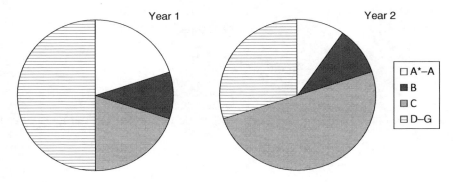

156 Select all the true statements:

    A. The proportion of pupils achieving A*–A improved in year two.

    B. The proportion of D–G grades remained the same.

    C. The proportion of pupils achieving A*–C grades improved in year two.

    D. We are not able to tell whether more pupils achieved a C and above in year two.

157 In year one, there were 130 pupils in Year 11. In year two, 30% of Year 11 achieved grades D–G from a total year group of 120. How many more pupils achieved grades D–G in year one than in year two?

As many as four pie charts might be given.

Practice questions

The pie charts show the proportions of levels achieved by pupils in one school at Key Stage 2.

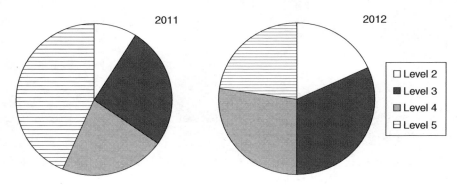

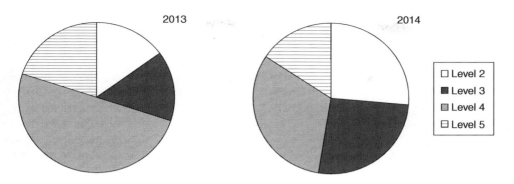

2013   2014

☐ Level 2
■ Level 3
▨ Level 4
⊟ Level 5

158 Point and click on the pie for the year which shows the best results for pupils achieving level 5.

159 Point and click on the pie for the year in which exactly half of the pupils achieve level 4 or 5.

160 A headteacher is reviewing the Key Stage 2 results of the Year 6 classes in four local schools. She produces the pie charts below.

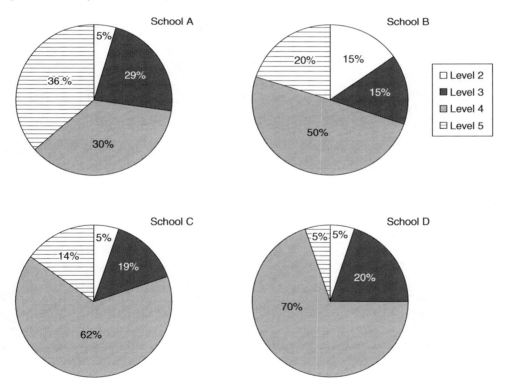

School A

5%
29%
36.%
30%

School B

20%   15%
15%
50%

☐ Level 2
■ Level 3
▨ Level 4
⊟ Level 5

School C

5%
14%
19%
62%

School D

5% 5%
20%
70%

What is the median percentage of pupils achieving level 4 and above in the four schools?

| 18.75 | 53 | 56 | 51.6 | 70 | 71.5 | 72.5 |

Bar charts

 Read carefully all titles: of the diagram and the axes. What does the data represent?

 A **bar chart** presents data as vertical or horizontal bars. The length of the bar indicates frequency of a data value.

Example

A survey was carried out to find the number of siblings per pupil in Year 6. The results are displayed in a bar chart:

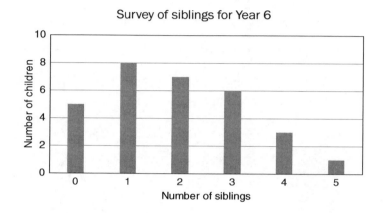

Survey of siblings for Year 6

What is the median number of siblings per child?

Reading from the vertical axis, total number of pupils = 5 + 8 + 7 + 6 + 3 + 1 = 30

 Read the vertical axis carefully. Here the 'number of children' are marked in 2s – so half way between is worth 1 child.

The 'middle' pupils are the 15th and 16th.

Considering the cumulative data:

Number of siblings	0	1	2	3	4	5	Total
Number of children	5	8	7	6	3	1	30
Cumulative frequency	5	13	20	26	29	30	

The 15th and 16th pupils appear in the third group, those with 2 siblings.

Answer: The median number of siblings is 2.

A simple bar chart can be used to illustrate categorical data or grouped data – see practice questions 161–169. More complex bar charts present two (or more) sets of bars against one axis as in practice question 170 and/or present stacked bars with each column showing the amounts (or share) of various subcategories within that data – see practice questions 171–180.

Practice questions

161 The French department wishes to compare their GCSE results with those from other departments. 75 pupils took French GCSE and 40 achieved grades A*–C.

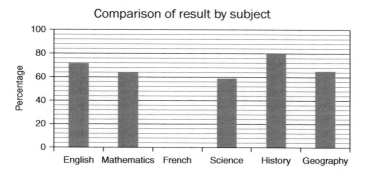

Comparison of result by subject

Select and place the correct bar onto the chart above.

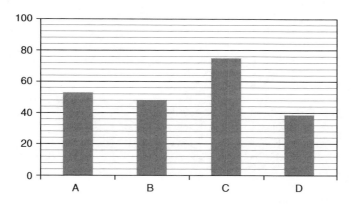

162 The Art department has analysed the percentage of GCSE grades A*–C over seven years.

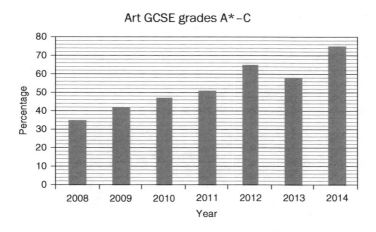

Art GCSE grades A*–C

Indicate all the true statement(s):

A. The mean percentage of GCSE grades A*–C for the first four years of the chart was 44% (to the nearest whole number).

B. The percentage of GCSE grades A*–C in 2008 was less than half of that in 2014.

C. The percentage of grades A*–C increased each year.

D. The median percentage of GCSE grades A*–C over the seven-year period was 51%.

More than one question might be set for a single simple bar chart.

Practice questions

A headteacher analysed unauthorised absence over half a term. She produced a bar chart to help with the analysis, looking at where pupils have taken a single day, or more than one consecutive day.

Analysis of consecutive days of unauthorised absences

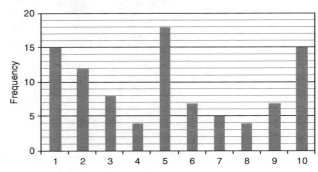

163 The total number of days' unauthorised absence is:

| 5 | 10 | 20 | 49 | 90 | 150 | 491 | 501 |

164 Select all the true statements:

A. The range of days of unauthorised absence is 10.

B. The modal number of consecutive days of unauthorised days of absence is 5.

C. The median number of consecutive days of unauthorised absence is 5.5.

The headteacher of a small primary school is concerned about the increase in unauthorised absences over a number of years. She compiles a bar chart to illustrate her concerns.

Analysis of unauthorised absences

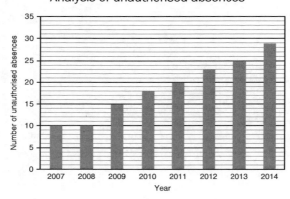

165 Point and click on the year that shows the greatest increase in unauthorised absences.

166 What is the mean number of unauthorised absences over the 8-year period? Give your answer to two decimal places.

167 What is the median number of unauthorised absences over the 8-year period?

| 10 | 17 | 18 | 19 | 20 |

A school offers three modern foreign languages for GCSE study. Pupils in Year 9 can choose to study one or two modern foreign languages. There are 104 pupils in Year 9. The diagram shows the choices made by those who chose to study two foreign languages:

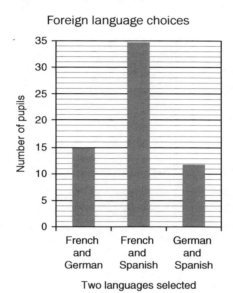

Foreign language choices

168 What proportion of the pupils in Year 9 has chosen to study two foreign languages? Give your answer as a decimal to one decimal place.

169 In addition, a further 25 pupils have chosen to study German at GCSE level as their only modern foreign language. What percentage of pupils will be studying German at GCSE?

| 24% | 30% | 45% | 50% | 60% | 84% |

To compare two (or more) sets of data, the bars can be set side by side for each data value on the x-axis. Read the legend to establish which bars relate to which data category.

Example

A geography class has 30 pupils. The teacher gives them a test at the beginning (test 1) and at the end (test 2) of the autumn term and compares the results.

Point and click on the test score where the greatest difference occurs between test 1 and test 2.

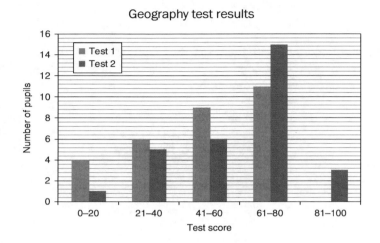

Geography test results

Reading the graph and tabulating the data gives:

	Test score				
	0–20	**21–40**	**41–60**	**61–80**	**81–100**
Test 1	4	6	9	11	0
Test 2	1	5	6	15	3
Difference	3	1	3	**4**	3

 The difference is found by subtraction: the smaller from the larger.

Visually, without having to do any calculation, the largest difference is seen by comparing heights of pairs of bar.

Answer: The greatest difference is in test score 61–80.

Practice question

170 Answer this question using the bar chart above. Indicate the true statement(s):

A. The overall results in test 2 were higher than in test 1.

B. The scores between 41 and 60 decreased in test 2 by one-third.

C. 85% of pupils scored more than 40% in test 2.

Single bars may be subdivided to show additional information about the data. The bars can be coded for different categories to show actual data values, one on top of another, or the share of the data.

For the upper part of a bar, calculate the length of that part of the bar by reading the upper and lower values and finding the difference.

Example

A headteacher is concerned about punctuality in the mornings and analyses methods of transport of a random sample of pupils across four different year groups.

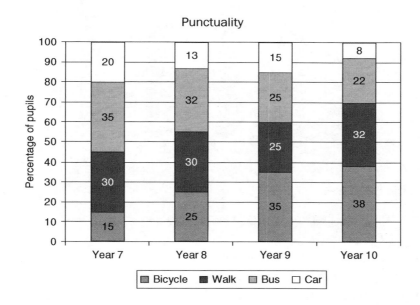

The ratio of pupils travelling to school by car to the number travelling to school by bus in its lowest terms is:

56:114   28:57   57:28   114:56

> Number travelling by car: 20 + 13 + 15 + 8 = 56
>
> Number by bus: 35 + 32 + 25 + 22 = 114

Answer: Ratio is 56:114 = 28:57.

56:114 is not correct because the simplified version is required.

Order matters with ratios. 28:57 is not the same as 57:28.

Practice questions

171 A comparison was made in the sixth form of one high school to determine the proportion of students who apply to university. The data was further broken down into gender, and bar charts produced.

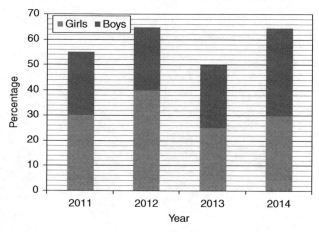

Proportion of girls and boys applying to university in a school's sixth form

Identify all the true statements:

A. In all four years, the proportion of girls applying to university is greater than the proportion of boys applying for university.

B. The highest proportion of boys applying for university was in 2012.

C. The highest proportion of all students applying for university was in 2012.

D. In each year, 50% or more of the students applied for university.

Five pupils took three advanced algebra tests after receiving extra mathematical support. Each test was marked out of 40. The bar chart shows a summary of their results:

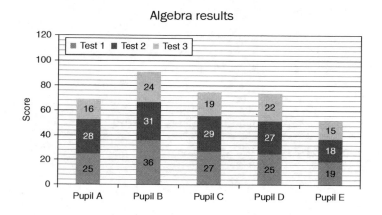

Algebra results

172 What is Pupil C's mean mark as a percentage to the nearest whole number?

173 Select all the true statements:

    A. The mean mark for test 1 is 25.

    B. The range of marks in test 3 is 9.

    C. The lowest mark was achieved in test 1.

    D. The modal mark over all three tests was 25.

Over a period of five years, Year 9 pupils in one high school had to select one technology subject to study to GCSE. Their selections are analysed to produce these composite bar charts:

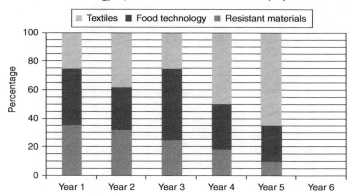

Technology option selections of Year 9 pupils

174 The popularity of *resistant materials* has decreased from year one to year five by:

    | 10% | 20% | 25% | 35% | 40% |

175 What is the median percentage of pupils choosing textiles as their technology option in years one to five?

176 In the sixth year, Year 9 pupils have just made their selections for the new academic year.

Subject	Resistant materials	Food technology	Textiles
% of pupils choosing that subject	30	30	40

Which of the bars below shows the data for the sixth year?

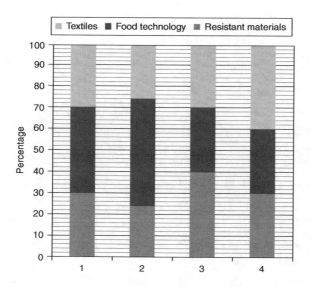

As part of a quality improvement initiative, three schools' senior management teams carried out classroom observations and made comparisons between the schools.

Quality improvement initiative: result of classroom observation

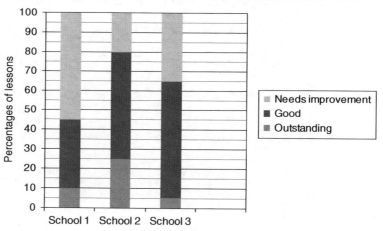

177 What is the mean percentage of lessons graded 'needs improvement' across the three schools? Give your answer to the nearest whole percentage.

178 Select the true statement(s):

A. In school 3, 65% were graded as 'Needs improvement'.

B. More than half the lessons in school 1 were graded 'Needs improvement'.

C. In school 2, $\frac{4}{5}$ of the lessons were graded 'good' or 'outstanding'.

179 In school 2, five lessons were graded as 'outstanding'. How many lessons observations were carried out in school 2?

| 6 | 10 | 20 | 25 | 50 | 100 | Not possible to tell |

180 A fourth school joins the comparison exercise. Their classroom observation grades are as follows:

Outstanding	Good	Needs improvement
15	75	10

Select the bar which represents this data.

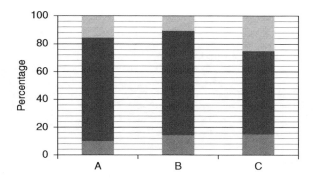

Read the axes carefully and be aware of the starting and ending values, the scale of the axes and the units for the data.

Graphs

Four types of graph appear in the numeracy skills test: scatter graphs, line graphs and cumulative frequency curves, and box and whisker diagrams.

All of these graphs present data pictorially, with points plotted against two axes: the vertical axis and the horizontal axis.

Scatter graphs

A scatter graph compares two paired sets of data by recording, as a single point, each pair. Each point represents, for example, one person.

Scatter graphs can be used to identify, for example, pupils whose performance is unusual or requires attention.

If the points on a scatter graph are clustered along a line, this indicates a relationship – correlation – between the two variables.

Perfect Positive Correlation	High Positive Correlation	Low Positive Correlation	No Correlation	Low Negative Correlation	High Negative Correlation	Perfect Negative Correlation

To compare one data set with the other, a line drawn joining points where the data is equal will separate the data into two subsets: one where one data reading is higher than the other and one where it is lower.

Example

Science and mathematics teachers are comparing test results for Year 10 pupils and plot a scatter graph to show the results.

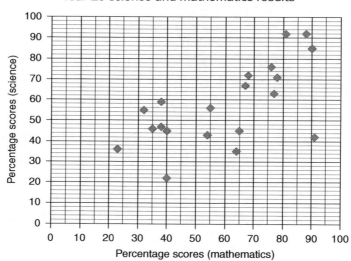

Year 10 science and mathematics results

Which points represent these pupils?

(a) *The pupil who scored the highest in mathematics*
Mathematics scores are on the horizontal axis. Look for the point furthest to the right.
Answer: (91, 42).

(b) *The pupil who came bottom in science*
Science scores are on the vertical axis. Look for the lowest point.
Answer: (40, 22).

(c) *The pupil who got between 50% and 60% in both tests*
Look between pairs of parallel lines at 50 and 60 from both axes.
Answer: (55, 56).

Practice questions

Using the scatter diagram above, now answer these practice questions.

181 Point and click on the pupil who has the greatest difference between their mathematics and their science scores.

182 The proportion of pupils who scored 50% or more in both subjects is:

| 50% | 0.45 | $\frac{8}{20}$ | Not able to tell |

Line graphs

Line graphs offer a visual representation of the relationship between two sets of related data. The axes are labelled with the data being measured (eg scores against years). Points are plotted and a line drawn to join these points, thus showing a **trend**.

Example

In a small primary school, Ofsted has praised the music teacher because the number of pupils in Year 6 learning a musical instrument has consistently risen over a four-year period.

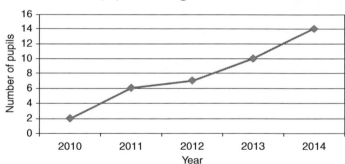

Number of pupils learning a musical instrument

There were 25 pupils in Year 6 in 2010 and 28 pupils in Year 6 in 2014. What is the percentage increase in pupils learning a musical instrument between 2010 and 2014?

Make sure the data for the correct years is used in the calculation.

2010: 2 pupils

$\frac{2}{25} \times 100\% = 8\%$

2014: 14 pupils

$\frac{14}{28} \times 100\% = 50\%$

50% − 8% = 42%

Answer: The percentage increase is 42%.

On one set of axes, more than one graph may be shown, so that a comparison between the two sets of data can be made.

Example

Two pupils' marks are compared in a series of mathematics tests.

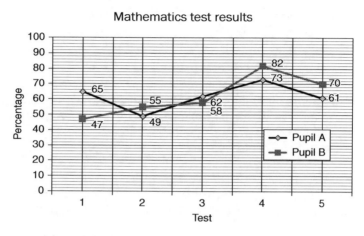

Mathematics test results

The mean difference between the pupils' marks is:

| 0.4 | 4 | 23 | 62 | 62.4 |

❌ Read the axes carefully and be aware of the starting and ending values, the scale of the axes and the units for the data.

For Pupil A:

Marks = 65 + 49 + 62 + 73 + 61 = 310

Average = $\dfrac{310}{5}$ = 62

For Pupil B:

Marks = 47 + 55 + 58 + 82 + 70 = 312

Average = $\dfrac{312}{5}$ = 62.4

Difference in averages = 62.4 − 62 = 0.4

Answer: The mean difference is 0.4.

OR

Difference between marks
= 18 + −6 + 4 + −9 + −9
= −2

Mean difference = $\dfrac{2}{5}$ = 0.4

More than one question might be set for a single graph.

Practice questions

The senior management team is making a comparison between the percentage of pupils achieving five A*–C grades at the end of Year 11 and the national averages over a six-year period.

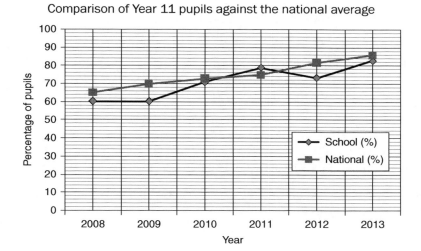

Comparison of Year 11 pupils against the national average

183 Point and click on the year when the school did better than the national average.

184 Select all the true statements:

   A. The school's highest percentage score was in 2011.

   B. 2010 was the year when the school made the greatest amount of improvement in percentage points.

   C. The percentage of pupils gaining five A*–C grades in the school fell in 2012.

   D. The school is performing consistently below the national average.

An art teacher is planning a school trip to an exhibition. She is making comparisons between two coach companies to obtain the best price.

○   The Dotty Coach Company charges a flat rate per trip of £200 and an additional cost per mile.

○   The Dashed Company charges £5 per mile.

She produces a graph (see overleaf) to show the difference between the prices of the two companies.

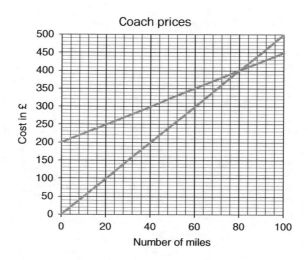

185 A third company charges £300 then £1 per mile. Point and click on the correct place on the graph to show where a journey of 100 miles would be if this company were to be used.

186 The distance between the school and the exhibition is 30 miles. What is the difference in the cost of this part of the journey for the Dotty and Dashed companies?

187 Select the true statement(s):

    A. For a distance of 20 miles, the Dotty Company charges £125 more than the Dashed Company.

    B. Both companies charge the same amount for a distance of 80 miles.

    C. The cost of hiring the Dashed Company for a journey of 120 miles is £600.

    D. The Dotty Company is cheaper for all journeys up to 60 miles.

Cumulative frequency curves

The cumulative frequency is the total number of data items up to a given data value. It can be plotted on a cumulative frequency graph, and this allows other information to be read from the graph, such as the median, and the upper and lower quartiles and hence the interquartile range. Having plotted a cumulative frequency curve, the data could be represented using a box and whisker diagram (page 82).

The cumulative frequency is always plotted on the vertical axis, with the graph curving from the bottom left to the upper right.

Example

A survey was carried out in one high school to determine how much time 150 pupils had spent watching television during the school week. How many watched more than 10 hours?

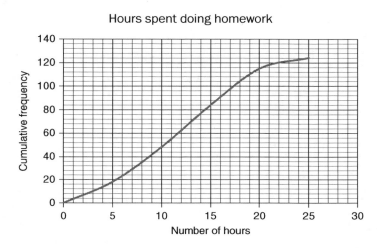

Time spent watching TV

Reading the graph up from 10 hours, the number of pupils is 40, but this shows the number who watched less than 10 hours.

Read the question carefully to determine whether you need to find 'more than' or 'less than' a particular value.

150 − 40 = 110

Answer: 110 pupils watched more than 10 hours' television during the school week.

Practice questions

A survey was carried out to determine how much time pupils in Year 7 spent doing homework per week. The results were plotted on a cumulative frequency graph.

Hours spent doing homework

188 How many pupils spent more than ten hours per week doing homework?

189 Select the true statements:

A. Altogether, 130 pupils took part in the survey.

B. Half the pupils did less than 15 hours per week.

C. Approximately 48 pupils did less than 10 hours per week.

D. Exactly 12 pupils did more than 20 hours per week.

Box and whisker diagrams

In a box and whisker diagram, the 'whiskers' show the complete range of the data, and the 'box' shows where half of the data lies. Often called a boxplot, the extent of the box is achieved by identifying the upper quartile and the lower quartile.

The box and whisker diagram therefore illustrates the spread of data (distance between the lowest and highest values), the median value (the middlemost value) and the upper and lower quartiles, and within the box, the interquartile range where half of the data lies.

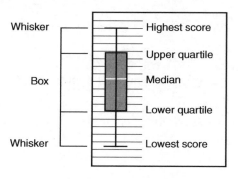

Read the axes carefully and be aware of the starting and ending values, the scale of the axes and the units for the data.

Practice question

190 The results of one class test are analysed and a boxplot produced.

The data summary is:

Lowest value	Lower quartile	Median	Upper quartile	Highest value
20	35	50	65	80

Point and click on the correct boxplot.

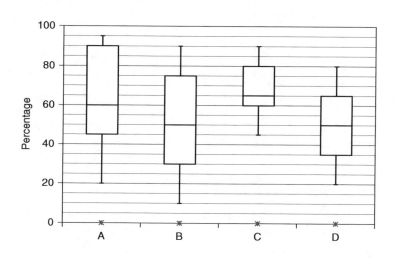

Several questions can be asked of the data presented in a single box and whisker diagram.

Practice questions

The history department set two tests for Year 10 pupils. The results are shown in the boxplots.

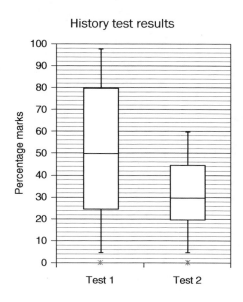

History test results

191 Forty-eight pupils took test 1. How many pupils scored between 50% and 80%?

192 Select all the true statements:

A. Many pupils found test 2 easier than test 1.

B. The interquartile range of test 1 is more than twice that of the interquartile range of test 2.

C. The range of marks for test 2 is 60.

D. 25% of the pupils gained 80% or more in test 1.

193 The marks for test 2 are standardised and all pupils' marks are increased by 13 percentage points.

The new interquartile range for test 2 is:

| 5 | 13 | 20 | 25 | 30 | 51 | 60 | 68 | 80 |

The diagram below shows the percentage test marks in English for two class groups.

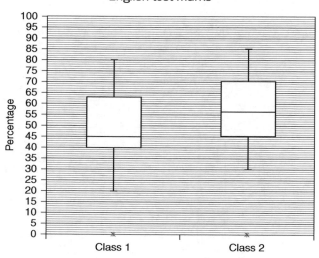

English test marks

194 What is the difference in the range of marks between the two classes?

195 The marks are standardised and all pupils' percentage marks in class 2 were reduced by 5%. What is the revised interquartile range for class 2?

| 20 | 22.5 | 23.75 | 25 | 40 | 42.75 | 52.25 | 55 | 51 | 66.5 |

Boxplots have been created to display the examination results for two Year 10 classes, each containing 28 pupils.

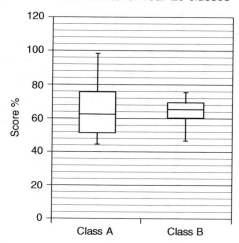

Test results for Year 10 classes

196 Indicate all the true statement(s):

   A. The range of marks for class B is lower than for class A.

   B. Fewer people in class A gained over 76% than in class B.

C. 21 pupils in class B scored 60 or more in the test.

D. Seven pupils in class A gained more than 80%.

197 The results for class C in Year 10 are summarised in the table below:

Lowest mark	Lower quartile	Median	Upper quartile	Highest mark
30	50	70	80	85

Select and place the correct boxplot into the chart above.

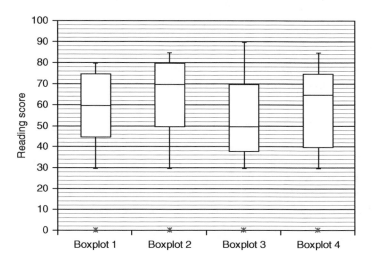

The reading ages of a group of pupils have been analysed over a three-year period. Boxplots have been created to show the results.

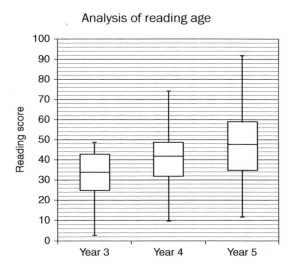

198 The maximum reading score is 100. The increase in the median score between year four and year five is:

| 3% | 6% | 14% | Not able to tell |

199 What is the difference in the interquartile range between year four and year five?

200 Select all the true statements:

  A. The median has increased by 16 points over the three-year period.

  B. There is a greater range of scores in year five than in either of the other two years.

  C. The interquartile range in year three is 18.

  D. All pupils have improved in reading over the three-year period.

Comparing box and whisker diagrams, say for the results of a series of tests, can lead to teachers asking questions about pupil performance and deciding on a course of action to address any issues identified.

○   If the tests were taken at approximately the same time, but on different topics, and the results vary widely, then perhaps some topics need to be revised more thoroughly.

○   If the tests were taken over a period of time, an improvement might be expected in the median score together with a reduction in the range.

Practice question

201 Boxplots were used to compare the test results of a year group over a period of time.

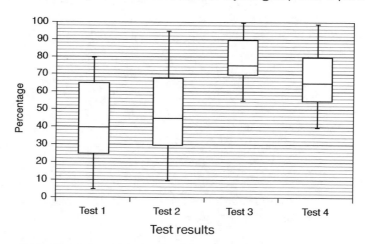

Click on the boxplot for the test which appeared to be the easiest.

3.5   Algebra

Algebra is the part of mathematics where letters are used instead of numbers.

Using simple formulae

A formula is a statement in words, or an equation using letters, to describe the relationship between two or more variables.

Example

One method of predicting A level results is to use a formula based on GCSE points.

   (21.71 × GCSE points score) − 44.69

What is a pupil's predicted A level points score for a pupil with a mean GCSE points score of 6.9? Give your answer to one decimal place.

Substitute the value 6.9 into the formula:

21.71 × 6.9 − 44.69

= 149.799 − 44.69

= 105.109

= 105.1 (to 1 dp)

Answer: The predicted A level points score for a pupil with a mean GCSE points score of 6.9 is 105.1 (1 dp).

Practice question

202 An internal test taken by 104 Year 8 pupils is marked by the relevant class teacher. The head of faculty then samples the marking to ensure consistency, according to a formula where n is the number of pupils taking the test.

$$\left(\frac{n}{10}\right) + 7$$

How many scripts must the head of faculty check?

When measuring temperature, there are two scales: Celsius or Fahrenheit. Using C as the temperature in degrees Celsius and F as the temperature in degrees Fahrenheit:

o   the formula to convert from Fahrenheit to Celsius is $C = (F - 32) \times \frac{5}{9}$

o   the formula to convert from Celsius to Fahrenheit is $F = C \times \frac{9}{5} + 32$

Practice question

203 The formula for changing °C to °F is

$$C = \frac{5(F - 32)}{9}.$$

What is 75°F in °C? Give your answer to the nearest whole number.

Weighting

Pupils sit two papers in an examination, Paper 1 and Paper 2, but their total mark is a combined weighted score. Paper 2 carries double the weight of Paper 1. Using S1 as the score on Paper 1 and S2 as the score on Paper 2, the total score S is given by

S = S1 + 2 × S2.

Example

For an end of year test, 25% of the marks were allocated to the practical work and the rest to the written paper. The practical was marked out of 30 and the written paper out of 120.

A pupil scored 15 for the practical and 95 for the written paper.

What was the pupil's final percentage mark? Give your answer to the nearest whole number.

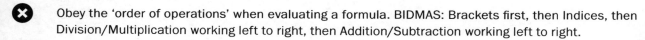

Obey the 'order of operations' when evaluating a formula. BIDMAS: Brackets first, then Indices, then Division/Multiplication working left to right, then Addition/Subtraction working left to right.

Practical: $\dfrac{15}{30}$ × 25% = 12.5%

Written: $\dfrac{95}{120}$ × 75% = 59.4%

Total mark: 12.5% + 59.4% = 71.9% = 72% to the nearest whole number

Retain the decimal places through the calculation. Round only at the very end.

Answer: The pupil's final mark is 72.

Practice questions

204 A pupil's final mark for a test is calculated as follows:

Part one × 0.6 + Part two × 0.4

To gain a grade A, a pupil needs a total score of 70 or more.

One pupil gains 65 marks in Part one. What is the lowest mark he must gain to be awarded an A?

205 A test is divided into two parts. 0.4 of the score of test 1 and 0.6 of the second test make up the final overall mark. A pupil scores 18 out of a possible 45 for the first test and 28 out of a possible 60 for the second. What is her overall mark as a percentage?

206 A test paper is made up of two papers. Paper 1 is worth 30% of the total and Paper 2 is worth 70% of the total amount.

Here are the results for two pupils.

Pupil	Paper 1 marked out of 80	Weighted score (%)	Paper 2 marked out of 65	Weighted score (%)
A	45	16.9	38	40.9
B	63		49	

Weighted scores are rounded to one decimal place. Drag and drop the correct amounts to complete the table.

22.6		23.6		23.7		52.7		52.8		55.1		75.3		78.8

207 Two exams are taken at the end of Year 10 in geography. The final score consists of 20% of the marks gained from the first paper and 80% of the marks gained for the second paper. A pupil scored 16 out of 40 for the first paper and 45 out of 80 for the second paper. What is the pupil's final score as a percentage?

208 An internal school examination is made up of three parts (tests a, b and c). A formula is then used to calculate each pupil's overall result:

$$\text{Final mark}\,(\%) = \frac{0.3a + 0.5b + 0.2c}{2.5}.$$

One pupil achieves the following results:

Test a	Test b	Test c
105	96	125

What is his overall percentage score? Give your answer to the nearest whole number.

Speed/time/distance

Some questions on the topic of time require you to use a formula to work out the time it will take to travel a given distance. The formula is:

distance = speed × time.

Example

A bus travels at 40mph. How far does it travel in 1.5 hours?

1.5 hours means $1\frac{1}{2}$ hours, ie 1 hour 30 minutes, not 1 hour 50 minutes.

Distance = 40 miles/hour × 1.5 hours = 60 miles

Answer: It travels 60 miles in 1.5 hours.

Practice questions

209 The venue for a school outing is 125 miles from the school. The students need to arrive at the venue at 11:00. The estimated mean speed of the coach is 50mph. What is the latest time the coaches must leave school?

210 A school sponsored walk is to cover 12km. Two breaks of 15 minutes each are planned and it is expected that the pupils will walk at an average of 5km per hour. They will start out at 09:00. At what time will they be expected to complete the walk?

211 A school trip to France is planned. The ferry is due to arrive in Calais at 11:15 and it normally takes a further 30 minutes to disembark. It is 48km from the ferry port to the hotel where the pupils will be staying. The average speed of the coach is estimated to be 45 miles per hour. At what time is the coach expected to arrive at the hotel? Use the conversion of 5 miles to 8km.

212 A party of school pupils is returning to the UK after staying in France. They need to be at the ferry port no later than 16:30. It is estimated that the coach will travel the 120km distance at an average speed of 50mph. What is the latest time they need to leave their accommodation? Use the conversion of 5 miles to 8km.

3.6   Numeracy practice papers

The answers to these questions appear on page 121–123.

Aim to complete each of these four papers under examination conditions.

Numeracy practice paper 1

Mental arithmetic questions

1   At a parents' evening, each interview is timed to last ten minutes. How long must the teacher allow in order to see twenty sets of parents? She is to have one break of fifteen minutes. Give your answer in hours and minutes.

2   A group of students decided to split the proceeds from a sponsored swim equally between three charities. The class raised two hundred and fifty-three pounds and five pence. How much will each charity receive?

3   Twenty-four pupils each pay two pounds fifty towards a school trip. How much money did the pupils pay in total?

4   The perimeter of the local park is one point two kilometres. A sponsored walk is planned for four circuits of the park. What is the total distance of the walk in kilometres?

5   A test is marked out of eighty. Pupils need sixty-five per cent for a grade A. How many marks is this?

6   As part of a school visit to Germany, pupils visited an exhibition. The total entrance fee was three hundred and sixty euros. What was the total entrance fee in pounds? Use the conversion of one euro equivalent to nought point eight pounds.

7   There are one thousand and seventy-four pupils in a high school. Two-thirds of the pupils have school meals at lunchtime. Each table in the dining room seats ten pupils. How many tables are needed?

8   A cross-country run covers three laps, each of two kilometres. The estimated speed of running is eight kilometres per hour. How long should the run take? Give your answer in minutes.

9   A high school's target for English GCSE results is that at least eighty per cent achieve grade C and above. How many pupils will need to achieve grade C and above from a cohort of two hundred and forty pupils in order to meet the target?

10   What is nought point four multiplied by seven point three?

11   A pupil achieves fifty-one out of sixty in a test. What is this as a percentage?

12   A primary school teacher estimates that his pupils will use six exercise books each during the school year. There are twenty-five pupils in his class. There are forty exercise books in a pack. How many packs must he order for the year?

Onscreen questions

1   A survey was carried out to find the number of siblings per pupil in Year 6. The results are displayed in a bar chart:

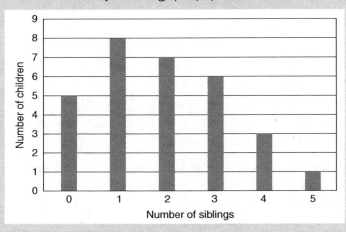

Survey of siblings per pupil in Year 6

What is the mean number of siblings per child? Give your answer to one decimal place.

2   A survey of the methods of transport used by a sample of staff at a high school is carried out. The results are:

	Bus	Car	Bicycle
Male	6	9	5
Female	8	7	1

What percentage of the staff cycle to the school? Give your answer to two decimal places.

3   A teacher analyses the results of the end of year tests for her German class. There were two tests – one oral and one written. The results are shown in the scatter graph.

Written versus oral results

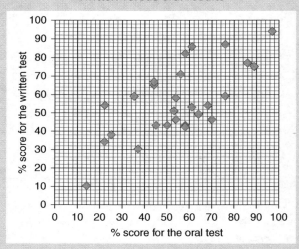

There were 28 in the German class. What proportion of pupils did better in the written test than in the oral test? Give your answer as a decimal to one decimal place.

4 A class teacher is looking at the attendance of his class over a five-week period. There are 28 children in the class.

	Mon	Tue	Wed	Thu	Fri	Total
Week 1		26	27	27	25	133
Week 2	25	26		22		123
Week 3	24	27	27	26	21	125
Week 4	22	24	28	25	26	125
Week 5	28		22	24	25	122
Total	127	126	130	124	121	628

Select and place the correct values in the table.

| 23 | 24 | 25 | 26 | 27 | 28 | 29 | 30 |

5 A pupil who plays in the school netball team will be selected to play for the county if her mean number of goals in seven matches exceeds 5. After six games, her mean score is 4.8 (to 1dp). What is the least number of goals she must score in the next game in order to be selected?

6 Boxplots were used to compare the test results of a year group over a period of time

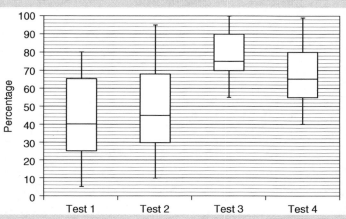

Test results

Indicate all the true statements:

A. Test 3 has the smallest range of marks.

B. Test 2 was found to be the most difficult.

C. The interquartile range for test 1 was 40.

D. Over half the pupils achieved over 65% in test 4.

7   42 pupils from Year 9 English groups and six teachers are going on an outing to see a play at the theatre. The group rate for theatre tickets is £15.55, with one free place for every 15 paid tickets. The train fare costs £18 per person. How much will each person have to pay for the outing? Give your answer to the nearest penny.

8   A school analyses its GCSE results in the core subjects of English, mathematics, science and a humanities subject. The results are summarised in the table below.

Grade	Number of pupils			
	English	Mathematics	Science	Humanities
A*–A	46	37	42	51
B–C	89	81	79	79
D–E	27	30	34	35
F–G	18	32	25	15

The English department has set a target of increasing the number of A*–C grades by 6% for the following academic year. Assuming there will be the same number of pupils taking GCSEs, how many more pupils will need to achieve grades A*–C?

9   A school analyses its GCSE results in the core subjects of English, mathematics, science and a humanities subject. The results are summarised in the table below.

Grade	Number of pupils			
	English	Mathematics	Science	Humanities
A*–A	46	37	42	51
B–C	89	81	79	79
D–E	27	30	34	35
F–G	18	32	25	15

What is the mean percentage of A*–A grades across the four core subjects to the nearest whole number?

| 21 | 23 | 24 | 25 | 26 | 29 |

10 A school governing body is looking at the age profile of the teachers in the school over a five-year period. The data is shown in the pie charts below:

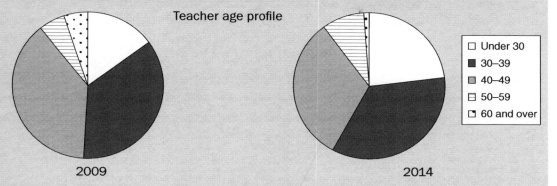

Teacher age profile

2009   2014

☐ Under 30
■ 30–39
▨ 40–49
☐ 50–59
⬚ 60 and over

Select all the true statements:

A. There are more teachers under the age of 30 in the school in 2014 than in 2009.

B. The age profile of the teachers in 2009 was generally younger than in 2014.

C. Approximately 75% of teachers in the school in 2009 were aged between 30 and 49 years.

11 Four pupils were given additional support in a mathematics class and their test results analysed over a period of time. The results were plotted on a line graph.

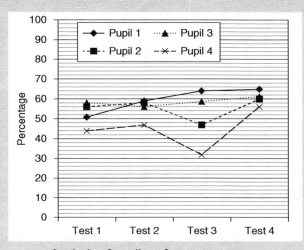

Analysis of pupil performance

Which pupil had the greatest range of marks?

12   This table shows the percentage score achieved by six pupils in an additional mathematics test.

Pupil	Percentage score
A	74
B	65
C	87
D	39
E	65
F	62

Select all the true statements:

A. The mode and the median are the same.

B. The mean is lower than the median.

C. The range is 48.

13   A learning support assistant used some new resources with a small group of pupils in a mathematics class. She tested the pupils before and after they used the new resources and analysed the results.

Pupil	Test results (%)		% difference
	Before	After	
A	55	69	
B	42	48	
C	69	55	
D	22	23	
E	44	56	

Point and click on the letter representing the pupil who made the most progress in terms of their % difference.

14   Pupils are attending a play at the theatre, which is 35 miles from the school. The play starts at 19:30. The teacher wishes to arrive at least 15 minutes before the start. It is estimated that the coach will be travelling at an average speed of 30 miles per hour. What is the latest time they must leave the school? Give your answer according to the 24-hour clock.

15 A survey of the methods of transport used by a sample of staff at a high school is carried out. The results are:

	Bus	Car	Bicycle
Male	6	8	6
Female	8	6	3

There are plans to build a car park for the school's 250 staff. Assuming that the above survey is representative of all staff, how many car-parking spaces are required to meet the current demand?

16 Year 11 form teachers are interested to determine how much additional study time their pupils undertook in the three-week period leading up to the GCSE examinations. The results are plotted on a cumulative frequency chart.

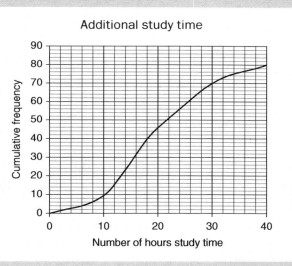

Additional study time

What is the median amount of additional study time undertaken by the Year 11 pupils?

15	18	20	22	40	80

Numeracy practice paper 2

Mental arithmetic questions

1   In a school of two hundred pupils, there are eighty pupils with English as an additional language. What proportion is this? Give your answer as a decimal.

2   A pupil scores eighteen out of twenty-five in one test and sixteen out of twenty in a second test. What is her average score across the two tests? Give your answer as a percentage.

3   In a sample of two hundred and twenty schools' Ofsted grades, thirty-three were graded as unsatisfactory. What fraction of the schools in the sample were graded unsatisfactory? Give your answer as a fraction in its lowest form.

4   A school purchases a new television set. The cost is two hundred and sixty pounds plus VAT at twenty per cent. What is the full cost of the television when VAT is included?

5   What is nought point three multiplied by five point seven?

6   A science experiment requires pupils to cut thin wire into lengths of nought point four five metres. The wire comes in five-metre rolls. How many pieces can be cut from one roll?

7   The national statistics for Key Stage 2 in mathematics showed that forty-four point three one per cent of pupils achieved level four and forty point six nine per cent achieved level five. What proportion of pupils achieved either level four or level five? Give your answer as a fraction.

8   The numbers of pupils in each class of a small primary school are: twenty, twenty-two, seventeen, nineteen and eighteen. What is the mean number of pupils per class? Give your answer to one decimal place.

9   A school's Key Stage 2 target for its sixty pupils in Year 6 is that at least seventy per cent will achieve a level four or above in mathematics. How many pupils must achieve a level four or above to meet the target?

10   In one term, a school employs a supply teacher for a total number of thirty-three days, costing one hundred and sixty pounds and fifty pence per day. What is the total cost of employing the supply teacher over the whole term?

11   A group of sixth formers are travelling to Japan. One Japanese yen equals nought point nought nought five pounds. How many Japanese yen will the students get for one hundred and fifty pounds?

12   A teacher is planning to show a documentary programme to his class. The programme lasts forty-seven minutes and he wants to allow at least fifteen minutes afterwards for discussion. The lesson finishes at eleven o'clock. What is the latest time he must start the documentary?

Onscreen questions

1   A junior school's daily lesson times are as follows:

09:15–10:45   11:05–12:30   13:20–14:20   14:30–15:30

How many hours and minutes per week are spent in lessons?

2   The test results for a group of pupils was recorded in the following table:

	Test 1	Test 2	Test 3	Test 4	Test 5
Pupil A	43	34	52	49	63
Pupil B	84	89	78	87	75
Pupil C	94	89	78	80	71
Pupil D	38	45	52	61	67

Indicate all the true statements:

A. The average mark for test 5 was higher than any other test.

B. The greatest range of marks was achieved in test 2.

C. The median mark for test 1 was 63.5.

D. Pupil A achieved the lowest mean score.

3   The test results for a group of pupils were recorded in the following table:

	Test 1	Test 2	Test 3	Test 4	Test 5
Pupil A	43	34	52	49	63
Pupil B	84	89	78	87	75
Pupil C	94	89	78	80	71
Pupil D	38	45	52	61	67

Pupil E's marks for the same test are as follows:

Test 1	Test 2	Test 3	Test 4	Test 5
86	92	76	58	72

What is the difference between the mean and median scores for all the pupils for test 4?

4   An end of year test in science uses the following formula to calculate the pupils' overall test scores:

$$\frac{M + 2P + 3W}{6}$$

M is the score for a multi-choice paper, P is the score for the practical and W is the score for the written test.

Three pupils' results were as follows:

Pupil	Test type		
	M	P	W
A	45	52	75
B	63	61	62
C	82	65	61

Point and click on the pupil who gained the highest score, using the formula.

5   The marks obtained by 60 pupils over two tests have been displayed in the following cumulative frequency charts:

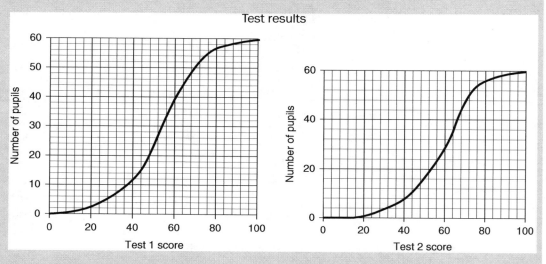

Indicate all the true statements:

A. The median mark for test 2 is higher than the median mark for test 1.

B. The interquartile range is higher in test 2 than in test 1.

C. 25% of pupils in test 1 obtained less than 40 marks.

D. The overall marks for test 2 are higher than for test 1.

6 As part of road safety week, pupils' bicycles were checked for faults. A table of results was compiled.

Number of faults	Number of bicycles
0	12
1	15
2	22
3	14
4	9
5	2
6	1

What is the mean number of faults per bicycle? Give your answer to the nearest whole number.

7 National statistics for attainment in the Key Stage 2 reading test in England are displayed in the line graph below (*Source*: www.gov.uk/government/collections/statistics-key-stage-2).

Attainment in Key Stage 2 reading test

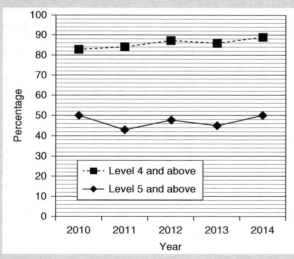

Select the true statements:

A. The percentage of pupils achieving level 4 and above has steadily increased over the last five years.

B. The best results of the last five years were achieved in 2014.

C. In 2011, 57% of pupils at Key Stage 2 achieved scores below level 4.

D. In 2010 and in 2014, half of all pupils achieved level 5 and above.

8   A Year 2 group is doing a project about looking after pets. The bar chart shows the number of pets each child has at home.

Pet survey

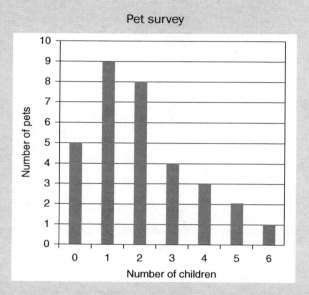

What is the mean number of pets? Give your answer to two decimal places.

9   A primary school headteacher has been given additional funding of £7054. She allocates the funding in the ratio of 3:4 between the infant and junior school classes. How much funding is allocated to the junior classes? Give your answer to the nearest whole £.

10   A French teacher compared the results of oral and written tests for a class of pupils.

French test results (percentages)

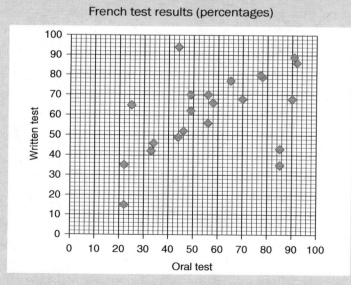

Point and click on the pupil who scored 50 points more on the oral test than on the written test.

11 A teacher is calculating the cost of a school trip to Sweden, based on 30 pupils. So far, she has estimated the following costs:

Transport (total)	£2352
Accommodation (total)	54,360 SEK
Food, sundries (per pupil)	1184 SEK

The currency conversion rate is £1 = 12.08 Swedish kroner (SEK).

Calculate the cost per pupil in pounds based on the teacher's estimates.

12 In mock GCSE examinations in a high school, 84 out of a possible 115 pupils achieved five A* to C grades. In the real GCSE examinations, 101 actually achieved five A* to C grades. What is this as a percentage increase? Give your answer to one decimal place.

13 The following table shows the pupil numbers by gender in three local primary schools.

	Number of boys	Percentage of boys	Number of girls	Percentage of girls	Total
School A	97	46	113	54	210
School B	56	52	52	48	108
School C	73	48	79	52	152

What is the average percentage of girls in the three schools? Give your answer to one decimal place.

14 A primary school with a total of 215 pupils has adopted a healthy-living initiative and has monitored how the children travel to school over a three-year period. The pie charts (two below and a third overleaf) show the results.

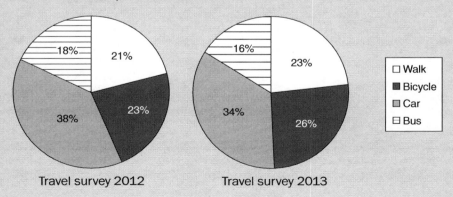

Travel survey 2012   Travel survey 2013

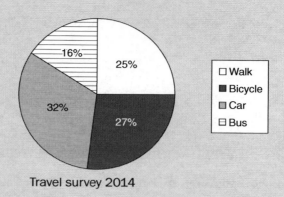

Travel survey 2014

How many more children either walk or go by bicycle to school in 2014 than in 2012?

15   The reading scores of two Year 6 classes are shown on the boxplots.

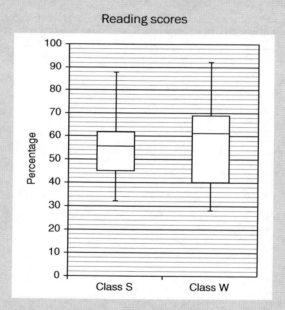

What is the difference between the two interquartile ranges?

16 Year 6 teachers at a primary school compared the results of the mathematics Key Stage 2 results.

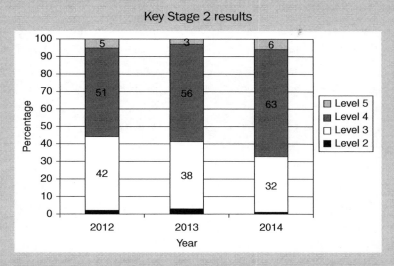

Key Stage 2 results

Year	2012	2013	2014
Number of pupils	32	35	28

How many more pupils achieved level 4 and above in 2014 compared to 2012?

Numeracy practice paper 3

Mental arithmetic questions

1 In a school, there are three hundred and fifteen pupils and fifteen teachers. What is the ratio of teachers to pupils? Give your answer as a fraction in its lowest form.

2 In one GCSE examination, nought point nought nought five pupils were ungraded. How many times more candidates did achieve a grade?

3 How much would it cost in pounds for thirty pupils to visit a museum in Germany at a cost of twenty euros per person? Use the exchange rate of one euro equals nought point eight pounds.

4 A new textbook costs eight pounds fifty pence. A teacher wants to buy forty and will receive a ten percent discount. What is the total cost of forty textbooks after the discount has been applied?

5 A primary school fete raises one thousand seven hundred and sixty-four pounds. The headteacher decides to allocate the money between the infant and junior schools in the ratio three to four. How much will be allocated to the junior school?

6   A high school records eighty-four unauthorised absences in one term. The headteacher wishes to reduce this by twelve per cent for the following term. What is the target number of unauthorised absences for the following term?

7   The school day starts at nine a.m. and finishes at four p.m. There are five lessons per day, each lasting one hour and five minutes. How much time is spent each day in other activities?

8   In a sponsored run, the mean number of laps completed by pupils was exactly six. The mean amount of money raised per lap was nine pounds. Thirty-eight pupils took part. How much money was raised in total?

9   Pupils are travelling to a concert sixty miles from the school. On the outward journey, the minibus driver estimates that the average speed will be forty-five miles per hour. How long will the journey take? Give your answer in hours and minutes.

10   Four out of nine teachers in a high school are male. There are sixty-three teachers in the school. How many are female?

11   The science department has spent four hundred and twenty-five pounds on new equipment from a budget of six hundred and seventy-five pounds. What proportion of the budget has been spent on new equipment? Give your answer as a fraction in its lowest terms.

12   Find the cost of fifty-two calculators each costing five pounds fifty pence.

Onscreen questions

1   A school's governing body is considering changes to the times of the school day. At present, school starts at 9:00 and finishes at 15:45, with total breaks of 1½ hours. The proposal is to start the school day at 08:45, finishing at 15:50, with the total break time being reduced to 1¼ hours. By how many minutes will the school day, excluding breaks, be increased?

2   The cumulative frequency chart shows the test results for Year 8 mathematics. How many pupils achieved 40 or more marks?

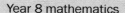

Year 8 mathematics

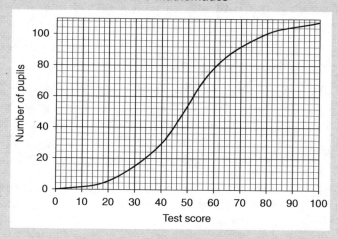

3 The art department of a high school buys card in sheets of A1, each of which has an area of 0.5m². The teacher needs to cut the card into size A4, with an area of 625cm². The teacher needs 30 pieces of A4 card. How many sheets of A1 will he need?

4 The cost of a school trip is summarised in the table below:

Coach hire	£250
Additional miles	45 @ 65p per mile
Entrance to museum	£4.50 per pupil, with one free place per 20 pupils

35 pupils are going on the trip. What is the cost per pupil?

5 The English and mathematics test scores of one year group are plotted on a scatter graph.

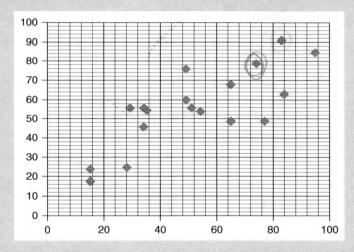

Point and click on the pupil who achieved the highest mean score over the two tests.

6 A pupil obtained the following marks in five tests:

Test A: $\dfrac{28}{35}$ Test B: $\dfrac{14}{20}$ Test C: $\dfrac{13}{30}$ Test D: $\dfrac{23}{30}$ Test E: $\dfrac{11}{15}$

What is her average mark as a decimal? Give your answer to two decimal places.

7 A technology department uses an estimate that $\dfrac{4}{11}$ of the allocated budget is spent on textbooks. Its departmental allocation for one year is £5654. How much does the department allocate to textbooks? Give your answer to the nearest pound sterling.

8 It is planned to create a new five-a-side football pitch in the school grounds. The pitch will measure 2500cm by 1650cm, with a border of 6m all the way round. What area of land is required in total to create the new pitch? Give your answer in m².

9   The bar chart shows the number of pupils on roll in Years 7 to 11.

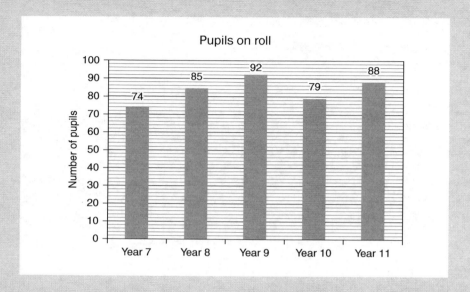

Select all the true statements:

A. The total number of pupils in Years 7 to 11 is 418.

B. The mean number of pupils per year group is 83 (to the nearest whole number).

C. The median number of pupils per year group is 85.

D. Approximately 21% of the pupils are in Year 11.

10 Following a heavy snowfall, many pupils in a rural primary school were unable to travel to school. The following table was compiled.

How many pupils did attend school that day?

Year group	Number on roll	Proportion of pupils absent
R	24	0.30
1	22	0.40
2	16	0.50
3	21	0.70
4	28	0.40
5	24	0.75
6	17	0.60

11 The following table shows the time taken by a small group of pupils to solve a mathematical problem.

Pupil	Time taken (mins:secs)
A	4:26
B	3:52
C	5:25
D	2:55
E	9:29
F	4:17

What is the mean time taken? Give your answer in minutes and seconds.

12 The results of an initial numeracy test given to all Year 7 pupils at one high school are recorded over a three-year period.

Results of initial numeracy test

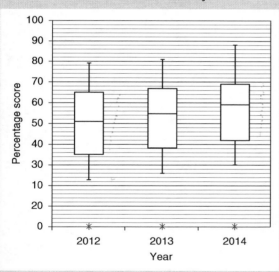

What is the difference in the interquartile ranges for 2012 and 2014?

13 A sponsored run took place on the school's 400m running track. The results were tabulated as follows:

Number of laps	Number of pupils
1	3
2	26
3	48
4	36
5	28
6	10
7	1

What is the total distance covered by all the pupils who took part? Give your answer in kilometres.

14 A sponsored run took place on the school's 400m running track. The results were tabulated as follows:

Number of laps	Number of pupils
1	3
2	26
3	48
4	36
5	28
6	10
7	1

What is the median number of laps completed?

15 One year, an awarding body had 2643 requests for a review of the grade awarded at GCSE in one subject. Of these, 59.4% resulted in a change of grade. How many reviews resulted in a change of grade?

16 A survey was made of 28 Year 7 and 35 Year 8 pupils into how much time they were spending playing computer games per day. The findings are shown in the pie charts below.

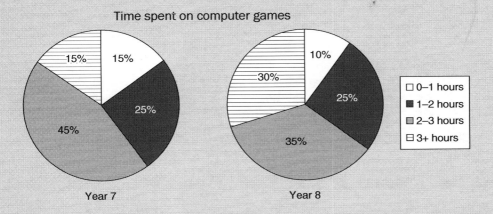

Time spent on computer games

Year 7

Year 8

0–1 hours
1–2 hours
2–3 hours
3+ hours

Select all the true statements:

A. Fewer Year 8 children spend more than three hours playing computer games per day than Year 7 children.

B. More than 50% of the Year 8 pupils surveyed play computer games for more than two hours per day.

C. Of the Year 7 children surveyed, only four play computer games for less than one hour per day.

Numeracy practice paper 4

Mental arithmetic questions

1 A new playing field has been created in the school grounds. It will be fifty-eight point five metres wide and seventy-five metres long. What is the area of the playing field? Give your answer in square metres.

2 A primary school with sixty pupils spends six thousand five hundred and twenty-five pounds on new resources. What is the mean amount spent per pupil?

3 In a charity events week, fourteen out of a total of three hundred and twenty-two pupils each raised more than one hundred pounds. What fraction of pupils raised more than one hundred pounds?

4 A class of pupils use different methods to estimate the height of a room. The highest estimate is six point nine metres and the lowest estimate is three point four two metres. What is the range of the estimates?

5 The ratio of male to female teachers in one primary school is seven to thirteen. What proportion of teachers is male? Give your answer as a decimal.

6 A school cross-country team did a series of practice runs. The first run was three kilometres, the second was four point five kilometres and the third was five point seven kilometres. What is the mean distance that the team ran over the practice sessions? Give your answer in kilometres and metres.

7 Pupils are supporting a charity by donating small boxes of gifts. They make up their own boxes from card. The boxes measure, in centimetres, thirty by twenty by fifteen. What is the volume of a box? Give your answer in cubic centimetres.

8 On a very foggy day, eighteen out of thirty pupils are late for school. What percentage of pupils arrived on time?

9 In GCSE English, nought point seven eight of the pupils achieved grade C or above in one high school. What fraction of the pupils did not achieve grade C or above? Give your answer as a fraction in its lowest form.

10 A group of technology students are researching obesity. One student states that his weight is twelve stones. What is this in kilograms? Use the conversion of one stone equals six point three five kilograms.

11 A high school's target for GCSE science is that at least seventy-six per cent of its pupils will achieve a grade C or above. One hundred and twenty pupils are taking GCSE science. How many must achieve a grade C or above for the school to meet its target?

12 A pupil took two tests. He achieved sixteen out of twenty in the first test and eighteen out of thirty in the second. What is his average score? Give your answer as a percentage.

Onscreen questions

1 A science group is following the instructions for a basic experiment where the expected temperatures have been given in degrees Fahrenheit.

The pupils have been given the formula to convert the temperatures to centigrade:

$$C = \frac{5(F-32)}{9}$$

Using this formula, convert 79°F to °C, giving your answer to the nearest whole number.

2 The Year 6 teachers examined the performance of their pupils midway through the year.

Level	1	2	3	4	5
Boys	2	4	9	6	1
Girls	1	3	5	8	3

What proportion of pupils gained level 4 and above? Give your answer as a fraction in its lowest terms.

3   A teacher offers after-school time slots to parents for consultations on two consecutive days. She allows 20 minutes per consultation and needs to make 16 appointments. She will start the sessions at 15:30 on the Monday and finish at 19:00 at the latest, with a break of 15 minutes at 17:30. Assuming she fills every slot consecutively, what time will she finish on the Tuesday evening?

4   The boxplots show the results of five tests taken by a class of geography students.

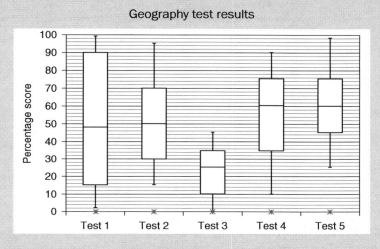

Geography test results

Point and click on the boxplot which best represents the following statement:

The test appeared to be too difficult for most of the students.

5   As part of a quality-improvement initiative, a school's senior management team carried out classroom observations in four different departments.

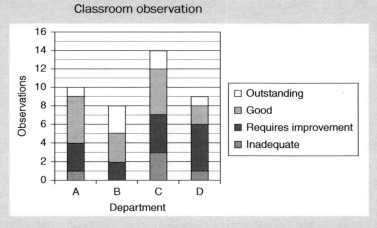

Classroom observation

What percentage of lessons was graded as 'good' across all four departments?

| 0.36% | 15% | 17% | 36.6% | 41% |

6 A new textbook is to be ordered. Each book costs £9.50. For orders over 50 in quantity, a discount of 15% can be applied. The teacher needs 45 books, but realises that it will be cheaper to order 50. What is the difference between the cost of 45 books and the cost of 50 books?

7 The final grade for a qualification, consisting of three parts, is calculated as follows:

Part A: 0.2; Part B: 0.3; Part C: 0.5

To obtain a pass, pupils must achieve an overall grade of 45 marks.

One pupil achieves 52 marks in Part A and 49 marks in Part B. What is the lowest mark she must achieve in Part C in order to obtain a pass?

8 The recommended classroom size for 25 pupils is 51m². Pupils measure the length and breadth of their classroom and note the following dimensions: 300 inches by 290 inches. They use the conversion of 2.5cm = 1 inch.

How much bigger is their classroom than the recommended minimum size? Give your answer in cm².

9 A Year 6 group has English lessons for 4¾ hours per week out of a total of 21¾ hours of lessons per week. What percentage of the weekly timetable is devoted to English? Give your answer to the nearest whole number.

10 Three sixth-form groups have set up business enterprises. Their total sales over a four-week period are displayed below.

Sales results

Select all the true statements:

A. The card-making enterprise took the highest amount of money over the four weeks.

B. The lowest sales were made by the pot-plant enterprise in week 4.

C. The range of sales totals is £37.

D. The mean sales total of the badge-making group is £50.58.

11 The dimensions of a piece of A4 paper are 210mm by 297mm. What is the area of a piece of A4 paper? Give your answer in cm².

12 A primary school's pupils' performance in reading in Key Stage 1 was tested and compared with the national averages.

Year	Percentage of boys at level 2 and above (school)	Percentage of boys at level 2 and above (national average)	Difference
2011	76.4	75.3	+ 1.1
2012	79.6	78.7	+ 0.9
2013	75.8	78.3	−2.5
2014	78.5	78.7	−0.2
			Mean difference:

Year	Percentage of girls at level 2 and above (school)	Percentage of girls at level 2 and above (national average)	Difference
2011	86.3	85.9	0.4
2012	87.4	86.2	1.2
2013	88.1	87.5	0.6
2014	89.2	87.4	1.8
			Mean difference:

Select and place the correct values, to one decimal place, for the mean differences.

| 0.7 | | −0.2 | | 0.2 | | 1.0 | | 1.2 | | 4.0 |

13 A comparison was made between four schools' Key Stage 2 results. The table shows the percentage of pupils out of the total number achieving level 4 or above, rounded to one decimal place.

School	2013	2014
A	77.8	78.7
B	76.4	79.9
C	81.5	83.4
D	75.5	79.2

What is the percentage increase in the mean between 2013 and 2014?

14 In one high school's sixth form, there were 76 school leavers in 2013 and 85 school leavers in 2014. The pie charts show the destinations of the school leavers over the two-year period.

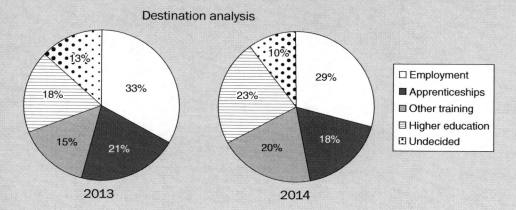

Destination analysis

2013

2014

Employment
Apprenticeships
Other training
Higher education
Undecided

How many more pupils were intending to go on to higher education in 2014 than in 2013?

15 A primary school's average points score for science at Key Stage 2 was 26.4. The following year it was 28.5. What is the percentage increase in the average point score? Give your answer to one decimal place.

16 The cost of a school trip for 20 pupils is summarised in the table:

Accommodation and meals (total)	€4400
Channel train	£75 per person
Entry fees to attractions (total)	£580
Sundries (total)	£675
Spending money	€50 per person

What is the estimated total cost per pupil in £?

Use the ratio £5 to €8.

Answers

Answers to numeracy practice questions

1	$\dfrac{7}{15}$	**15**	$\dfrac{2}{5}$	**29**	55%
2	$\dfrac{3}{5}$	**16**	$\dfrac{17}{20}$	**30**	357
				31	£35.75
3	$\dfrac{5}{32}$	**17**	$\dfrac{7}{20}$	**32**	£50
4	228	**18**	18	**33**	A
5	108	**19**	$\dfrac{3}{10}$	**34**	0.7
6	15			**35**	0.67
7	$\dfrac{1}{4}$	**20**	$\dfrac{7}{40}$	**36**	0.6
		21	32	**37**	0.35
8	236	**22**	$\dfrac{13}{20}$	**38**	$\dfrac{1}{5}$
9	$\dfrac{1}{12}$	**23**	$\dfrac{9}{20}$	**39**	$\dfrac{4}{7}$
10	252			**40**	28:29
11	9	**24**	739	**41**	£182
12	63	**25**	33%	**42**	£525
13	332.85	**26**	17%	**43**	£74.40
14	$\dfrac{13}{20}$	**27**	53%	**44**	£36
		28	20%	**45**	£19.50

46	£150	74	37.5^2	103	8.5km
47	£95.09	75	$43.5m^2$	104	22
48	£133.30	76	$4m^2$	105	12
49	£30	77	$733.5m^2$	106	10.2km
50	€35	78	4m	107	76
51	£300	79	40ml	108	40.7
52	255 Canadian dollars	80	30 litres	109	7.6
53	£15	81	$20cm^3$	110	22 months
54	£357.21	82	$33750cm^3$	111	−2°C
55	12,500 krona	83	20 miles	112	8°C
56	£21.67	84	227g	113	Week 1
57	£212.55	85	1.5m	114	4.1
58	£14	86	15°C	115	A, C and D
59	5 hours	87	50762	116	2.45 seconds
60	23 hours + 20 minutes	88	22:93	117	B and C
61	110 minutes	89	55°C	118	A and D
62	4 hours 20 minutes	90	£78	119	A and C
63	21:58	91	11.25 litres	120	Week 3
64	2km	92	2600m	121	45 minutes
65	100	93	50%	122	0.6
66	14.4km	94	61	123	$\frac{9}{50}$
67	14	95	11 years 7 months	124	0.6
68	328.1km	96	0.4°C	125	$\frac{17}{40}$
69	2.6 miles	97	0.62	126	18
70	20.5km	98	£9.25	127	Pupil C: −4; Pupil D: +1; Pupil E: +12
71	$24m^2$	99	£955.50		
72	54m	100	53%	128	$\frac{19}{23}$
73	50m	101	13		
		102	1		

129

Level 3	Level 4	Level 5
6	8	4
33	44	22
6	12	6
25	50	25
7	16	9
22	50	28

130 6, 3, 5

131 63% to the nearest whole %

132 (Year 3) 76.5%

133 2012

134 44

135 68%

136 Class (2) 27%

137

English	Mathematics	Science	Humanities
45	42	52	57
88	79	67	**74**
56	**49**	52	46
22	41	40	34
211	211	211	211

English	Mathematics	Science	Humanities
63	**57**	56	27
90	81	**81**	84
100	100	100	100

138 13

139 Pupils D and E

140 All statements are true

141 0.2

142 B, C and D

143

Boys:

2015	79.1	78.9

Girls:

2015	89.8	87.6

144 Pupil F

145 A, B, C and E

146 A and B

147 $\frac{11}{17}$

148 0.5

149 A and B

150 51

151 1

152 A

153

	N	M	S	C	F
7	25	15	25	15	20
10	30	10	35	5	20

154 70

155 B and C

156 C and D

157 29 pupils

158 2011

159 2012

160 72.5

161 A

162 A, B and D

163 491

164 B

165 5 is the greatest increase, in 2009

166 18.75

167 19

168 0.6

169 50%

170 A and B

171 D

172 63%

173 B

174 25%

175 35

176 Column 4

177	37%	**190**	D	**203**	24°C
178	B and C	**191**	12 pupils	**204**	78
179	20	**192**	B and D	**205**	44%
180	B	**193**	25	**206**	23.6% and 52.8%, respectively
181	(91, 42)	**194**	5	**207**	53%
182	0.45	**195**	25	**208**	42
183	2011	**196**	A and C	**209**	08:30
184	B and C	**197**	2	**210**	11:54
185	(100, 400)	**198**	6	**211**	12:25
186	£125	**199**	7	**212**	15:00
187	B and C	**200**	B and C		
188	76	**201**	Test 3		
189	B and C	**202**	17		

Answers to numeracy practice papers

Numeracy practice paper 1

Mental arithmetic questions

1	3 hrs 35 mins	**5**	52	**9**	192
2	£84.35	**6**	£288	**10**	2.92
3	£60	**7**	72	**11**	85%
4	4.8km	**8**	45 mins	**12**	4

Onscreen questions

1   1.9
2   16.67%
3   0.4
4   Mon. wk 1: 28; Tue. wk 5: 23; Wed. wk 2: 26; Fri. wk 2: 24
5   6
6   A, C and D
7   £32.58
8   11
9   24%
10 A and C
11 Pupil 4
12 A and C
13 A
14 18:05
15 95
16 18 hours

Numeracy practice paper 2

Mental arithmetic questions

1   0.4
2   76%
3   $\frac{3}{20}$
4   £312
5   1.71
6   11
7   $\frac{17}{20}$
8   19.2
9   42
10 £5296.50
11 30,000 Yen
12 9:58

Onscreen questions

1   24 hrs 35 mins
2   C and D
3   6
4   C
5   A and D
6   2
7   B and D
8   2.03
9   £4031
10 (85, 35)
11 £326.41
12 14.8
13 51.9%
14 17
15 12
16 1

Numeracy practice paper 3

Mental arithmetic questions

1   1:21
2   199
3   £480
4   £306
5   £1008
6   74
7   1 hr 35 mins
8   £2052
9   1 hr 20 mins
10 35
11 $\frac{17}{27}$
12 £286

Onscreen questions

1 35 mins	**7** £2056	**13** 220km
2 78	**8** 1054.5m²	**14** 3
3 4	**9** A, C and D	**15** 1570
4 £12.35	**10** 74	**16** B and C
5 (96, 85)	**11** 5:04	
6 0.69	**12** 3	

Numeracy practice paper 4

Mental arithmetic questions

1 4387.5m²   **5** 0.35   **9** $\frac{11}{50}$

2 £108.75   **6** 4km 400m   **10** 76.2kg

3 $\frac{1}{23}$ **7** 9000cm²   **11** 91

4 3.48m   **8** 40%   **12** 70%

Onscreen questions

1 26°C   **7** 40   **13** 2.5%

2 $\frac{3}{7}$ **8** 33,750cm²   **14** 6

3 18:05   **9** 22%   **15** 8.0%

4 Test 3   **10** C   **16** £306.50

5 36.6%   **11** 623.7cm²

6 £23.75   **12** −0.2, 1.0

Show me: solutions to numeracy practice questions

1 14 out of 30 = $\frac{14}{30}$ = $\frac{7}{15}$

2 Number of boys: 2 + 3 + 4 + 5 + 1 = 15

Number of boys at levels 3 or 4: 4 + 5 = 9

$$9 \text{ out of } 15 = \frac{9}{15} = \frac{3}{5}$$

3 $\frac{1}{4}$ of $\frac{5}{8} = \frac{1}{4} \times \frac{5}{8} = \frac{5}{32}$

4 $\frac{1}{4}$ of $342 = 342 \div 3 = 114$

$\frac{2}{3}$ of $342 = 114 \times 2 = 228$

5 $\frac{1}{8}$ of pupils $= \frac{288}{8} = 36$

$\frac{3}{8}$ of pupils $= 36 \times 3 = 108$

6 4 out of 9 are girls

5 out of 9 are boys

$\frac{5}{9}$ of $27 = 5/9 \times 27 = 15$

7 45 out of $180 = 45/180 = \frac{1}{4}$

8 $\frac{1}{4}$ did not attend; $\frac{2}{3}$ did attend

$\frac{1}{4}$ of $354 = 118$

$\frac{2}{3}$ of $354 = 236$

Read the question carefully. Watch out for negatives such as 'are <u>not</u> able'.

9 Cat: $\frac{1}{4}$ of $48 = 12$

Dog: $\frac{1}{4}$ of $12 = 4$

4 out of $48 = \frac{4}{48} = \frac{1}{12}$

To find a fraction of a fraction, multiply the fractions together: $\frac{1}{4}$ of $\frac{1}{4} = \frac{1}{4} \times \frac{1}{3} = \frac{1}{12}$.

10 0.6 of $420 = 0.6 \times 420 = 252$

11 0.3 of $30 = 0.3 \times 30 = 9$

12 0.7 of $210 = 147$

$210 - 147 = 63$

Read the question carefully. Watch out for negatives such as 'did <u>not</u> take part'.

13 332.85

14 $0.65 = \dfrac{65}{100} = \dfrac{13}{20}$

15 $0.4 = \dfrac{4}{10} = \dfrac{2}{5}$

16 $0.85 = \dfrac{85}{100} = \dfrac{17}{20}$

17 $0.35 = \dfrac{35}{100} = \dfrac{7}{20}$

18 40% girls; 60% boys

60% of 30 = 0.6 × 30 = 18

19 $30\% = \dfrac{30}{100} = \dfrac{3}{10}$

20 $17.5\% = \dfrac{175\%}{10} = \dfrac{175}{1000} = \dfrac{7}{40}$

21 70% of 45 = 0.7 × 45 = 31.5

Round up as 31 is not enough to pass.

22 $65\% = \dfrac{65}{100} = \dfrac{13}{20}$

23 100% − 55% = 45%

$45\% = \dfrac{45}{100} = \dfrac{9}{20}$

24 Absent: 2.5% of 960 = 0.025 × 960 = 24

Exams: 15.2% of 960 = 0.152 × 960 = 146

Trip: 5.3% of 960 = 0.053 × 960 = 51

In lessons: 960 − (24 + 146 + 51) = 739

25 14 out of 42 = $\dfrac{1}{4}$

$= \dfrac{1}{4} \times 100\% = 33\dfrac{1}{4}\%$

= 33% to the nearest whole number

26 $4\dfrac{1}{2} = 4.5$

4.5 out of 27 as a percentage

$= 4.5 \div 27 \times 100\%$

= 9 ÷ 54 × 100%

= 17% to the nearest whole number

Double top and bottom $\left(\dfrac{9}{54}\right)$.

27 16 out of 30 as a percentage = 16 ÷ 30 × 100% = 53% to the nearest whole number

28 6 out of 30 as a percentage = 6 ÷ 30 × 100% = 20% to the nearest whole number

29 33 out of 60 as a percentage = 33 ÷ 60 × 100% = 55%

30 15% receive school meals

15% of 420 pupils = 63

Number not receiving free school meals = 420 − 63 = 357

Read the question carefully. Watch out for negatives such as 'not'.

31 100% − 45% = 55%

55% of £65 = 0.55 × £65 = £35.75

32 100% − 70% = 30%

£15 is 30% of total cost

$£\dfrac{15}{30}$ is 1%

$£\dfrac{15}{30} \times 70 = £35$

£35 + £15 = £50

33 Statement A: Less than 80% of the pupils had a reading age below that of their actual age.

Number of pupils = 6

Pupils with reading age below their actual age: 1, 3, 4, and 5

Number of pupils with reading age below their actual age = 4

4 out of 6 = $\dfrac{4}{6} \times 100\% = 67\% < 80\%$

Statement A is true.

Statement B: Pupil 3 had 40% lower reading age compared to his actual age (to the nearest whole month).

Pupil 3's actual age = 10 × 12 months + 8 months = 128 months

Pupil 3's reading age = 8 × 12 months + 3 months = 99 months

Difference = 128 months − 99 months = 29 months

29 out of 128 = $\dfrac{29}{128} \times 100\% = 22.6\%$

Statement B is not true.

Statement C: 50% of the pupils had a reading age of at least 1 year 6 months below the actual age.

Only pupil with reading age at least 1 year 6 months below the actual age is Pupil 3.

1 out of 6 = 1/6 × 100% = 17% ≠ 50%

Statement C is not true.

34   28 out of 40 = $\dfrac{28}{40} = \dfrac{7}{10} = 0.7$

35   16 out of 48 = 1 out of 3 = 0.33   OR

  1 − 0.33 = 0.67 $48 - 16 = 32$

                                         $\dfrac{32}{48} = \dfrac{2}{3} = 0.67$

Read the question carefully. Watch out for negatives such as 'not'.

36   75 out of 125 = 75 ÷ 125 = 3 ÷ 5 = 0.6

37   7 out of 20 = 7 ÷ 20 = 0.35

38   5 recordings of 0°C.

  5 out of 25 = $\dfrac{5}{25} = \dfrac{1}{5}$

39   Number < level 4:

  2 + 3 + 4 + 0 + 2 + 5 = 16

  Total number of pupils:

  16 + 5 + 1 + 6 + 0 = 28

  Proportion:

  16 out of 28 = $\dfrac{16}{28} = \dfrac{4}{7}$

40   Total boys = 28 + 25 + 31 + 28 = 112

  Total girls = 32 + 29 + 26 + 29 = 116

  Ratio of boys to girls = 112:116

  Dividing both by 4, gives, in lowest terms, the ratio as 28:29

41   28 × £6.50 = £182

42   150 meals × £3.50 per meal = £525

43   6 miles × £12.40 per mile = £74.40

44   200 copies × 6 pages per copy = 1200 pages

  1200 pages × 3p per page = 3600p = £36

45 $50 \times 0.3 \times £1.30 = £19.50$

46 $\dfrac{5}{8}$ of £240 = £150

47 $\dfrac{1}{3}$ of £456.42 = $£\dfrac{456.42}{3}$ = £152.14

$\dfrac{5}{8}$ of £152.14 = $\dfrac{5}{8} \times £152.14$ = £95.09 (nearest penny)

48   5 March:

2×45 miles = 90 miles

90 miles @ 45p/mile = £40.50

19 March:

2×36 miles = 72 miles

72 miles @ 45p/mile = £32.40

26 March:

2×6 miles = 12 miles

12 miles @ 45p/mile = £5.40

£5.40 + £45.50 + £9.50 = £60.40

Total cost:

£40.50 + £32.40 + £60.40 = £133.30

49   Student ticket price: $0.85 \times £20 = £17$

Total ticket price: $(3 \times £20) + (30 \times £17) = £60 + £510 = £570$

Total cost of trip: £570 + £412.50 = £982.50

£982.50 ÷ 33 = £30 (to the nearest whole pound)

50   £25 = $25 \times €1.40$ = €35

€1.40 = £1

51   1 cedi = £0.2; 1500 cedi = $1500 \times £0.2$ = £300

52   £1 = 1.7CAD; £150 = 150×1.7CAD = 255CAD

53   €360 ÷ 20 = €18

£1 = €1.20; €1 = £1/1.2

€18 = £18 ÷ 1.20 = £180 ÷ 12 = £15

54   US$1 = £0.63; US$567 = $567 \times £0.63$ = £357.21

55   1 krona = £0.0052; £1 = $\dfrac{1}{0.0052}$ krona

£65 = 65/0.0052 krona = 12,500 krona

56   £4 = €5

£1 = €(5 ÷ 4)

For the spending money: £60 = 60 × 5 ÷ €4 = €75

€75 − €50 = €25

For the €25 remaining: €15 = £13

€1 = £13 ÷ 15

€25 = 25 × £13 ÷ 15 = £21.67

57   £5 = €8

$€1 = £\dfrac{5}{8}$

Total accommodation: €1750 = $1750 \times £\dfrac{5}{8}$ = £1093.75

Accommodation per pupil = $£\dfrac{1093.75}{25}$ = £43.75

Train cost per pupil: £69

Entry fees per pupil = $£\dfrac{1000}{25}$ = £40

Sundries per pupil = $£\dfrac{870}{25}$ = £34.80

Spending money per pupil: €40 = $40 \times £\dfrac{5}{8}$ = £25

Total per pupil = £43.75 + £69 + £40 + £34.80 + £25 = £212.55

58   Belgium exchange £1 = €1.23

Euros taken: £75 = 75 × €1.23 = €92.25

€92.25 − €76 = €16.25

Return exchange £1 = €1.17; $€1 = £\dfrac{1}{1.17}$

€16.25 = $16.25 \times £\dfrac{1}{1.17}$ = £13.88 = £14 (to nearest pound)

59   6 × 50 minutes = 300 minutes

300 minutes ÷ 60 minutes/hour = 5 hours

60   5 days in the week

Hours: 5 × 4 hours = 20 hours

Minutes: 5 × 40 minutes = 200

200 minutes ÷ 60 minutes/hour = $3\dfrac{1}{4}$ hours = 3 hours 20 minutes

20 hours + 3 hours + 20 minutes = 23 hours + 20 minutes

61 Total mathematics time = 4 hours 20 minutes = 4 × 60 minutes + 20 minutes
= 260 minutes

Teacher-led = 2 hours 30 minutes = 2 × 60 minutes + 30 minutes = 150 minutes

260 − 150 = 110

62 $\frac{1}{3}$ of 6 hours 30 mins = 2 hours 10 mins

6 hours 30 mins − 2 hours 10 mins = 4 hours 20 mins

OR

$\frac{2}{3}$ of 6 hours 30 mins = 2 × 2 hours 10 mins = 4 hours 20 minutes

63 12 × 8 minutes = 96 minutes of musical items

10% of 20 minutes = 2 minutes

20 minutes + 2 minutes = 22 minutes' break

10 × 3 minutes = 30 minutes setting up

Total time = 96 + 22 + 30 = 148 minutes

19:30 + 2 hours and 28 mins = ...

Time to finish = 21:58

64 Perimeter = 600m + 400m + 600m + 400m = 2000m = 2km

65 8.3 × 2 × 6 = 99.6 = 100 to the nearest mile

66 10 times per lesson: 10 × 90m = 900m in one lesson

16 lessons per week: 16 × 900m = 14,400m in one week

14,400m = 14.4km

67 1.03m = 1.03 × 100cm = 103cm

Change to centimetres first.

103cm ÷ 7cm = 14.7 (to 1 dp) = 14 (rounded down to the nearest whole number)

68 Total number of laps: (3 × 3) + (4 × 4) + (18 × 5) + (13 × 6) = 9 + 16 + 90 + 78 = 193

193 laps of 1700m/lap = 328,100m

$328,100m = \frac{328,100}{1000}$ km = 328.1km

69 $\frac{1}{4} + \frac{1}{8} + \frac{2}{5} = \frac{103}{120}$ OR $\frac{1}{4}$ of 18 = 6 (flat)

$\frac{17}{120} \times 18 = 2.6$ $\frac{1}{8}$ of 18 = 2.25 (forest)

$\frac{2}{5}$ of 18 = 7.2 (uphill)

Mixed: 18 − 6 − 2.25 − 7.2 = 2.55 = 2.6 to 1 dp

70 Total distance on map:

1.4cm + 5.6cm + 3.9cm + 7.4cm + 2.2cm = 20.5cm

Ratio 1:100,000

20.5cm: 20.5 × 100,000cm

Length is 2,050,000cm = 20.5km

71 600cm × 400cm = 6m × 4m = 24m²

72 4860m² ÷ 90m = 54m

73 6000m² ÷ 120m = 50m

74 Area of trapezium = average depth × length

$$= \frac{(1m+2m)}{2m \times 25m}$$

= 1.5m × 25m

= 37.5m²

OR

Rectangle measuring 25m × 1m = 25m²

Plus triangle = $\frac{1}{2}$ × 25m × 1m = 12.5m²

Area of trapezium = 25m + 12.5m = 37.5m²

75 Perimeter = 10m + 9m + 10m + 9m = 38m

Losing 9m for doors etc, leaves 38m − 9m = 29m around the walls

Available area = 29m × available height

Available height = 2m − 0.5m = 1.5m

Available wall space = 29m × 1.5m = 43.5m²

76 Lawn area = 6m × 10m = 60m²

Area of 1 rectangle for counting purposes = 60m² ÷ 15 = 4m²

77 Method 1: Calculating the overall rectangle and subtracting the two cut-outs

Top right cut-out rectangle is 32m by (25 − 10.5)m

Bottom left cut-out rectangle is 5m by 10.5m

50m × 25m − (5m × 10.5m) − (32m × 14.5m)

1250m² − 52.5 m² − 464m² = 733.5m²

Method 2: Dividing the area into two rectangles

14.5 × 18 + 45 × 10.5 = 733.5

78 $224m^3 \div 8m \div 7m = 4m$

79   3 litres = 3000ml

Change to millilitres first.

$3000ml \div 75 = 40ml$

80 $50cm \times 30cm \times 20cm = 30,000cm^3$

$1000cm^3 = 1$ litre

$30,000cm^3 = 30$ litres

81   Acid : water $= 2:50 = \dfrac{2}{50}: 1$

Water : acid $= 1:\dfrac{2}{50}$

$\dfrac{1}{2}$ litre: $\dfrac{2}{50} \times \dfrac{1}{2}$ litre

$\dfrac{2}{50} \times \dfrac{1}{2}$ litre $= \dfrac{1}{50}$ litre

1 litre = $1000cm^3$

$\dfrac{1}{50} \times 1000cm^3 = 20cm^3$

82 $1'' = 2.5cm$

Convert first.

$12'' = 12 \times 2.5cm = 30cm$

$15'' = 15 \times 2.5cm = 37.5cm$

$30cm \times 30cm \times 37.5cm = 33,750cm^3$

OR

$12'' \times 12'' \times 15'' = 2160$ cu in

$2.5cm = 1''$

$2.5cm \times 2.5cm \times 2.5cm = 1$ cu in

2160 cu in $= 2160 \times 2.5 \times 2.5 \times 2.5cm^3 = 33,750cm^3$

83   5 miles $\cong$ 8 kilometres

1 kilometre $= \dfrac{5}{8}$ miles

32 kilometres $= 32 \times \dfrac{5}{8}$ miles $= 20$ miles

84 1 oz $\cong$ 28.4g

8oz = 8 × 28.4g = 227.2g = 227g to the nearest gram

85 30cm $\cong$ 1 foot

5 feet = 5 × 30cm = 150cm = 1.5m

86 59 − 32 = 27

27 × 5 = 135

$\dfrac{135}{9}$ = 15

87 UK travel: 2 × 165 miles = 330 miles

French travel: 2 × 144km + 192km = 288km + 192km = 480km

8km = 5 miles; 1km = $\dfrac{5}{8}$ miles

480km = 480 × $\dfrac{5}{8}$ miles = 300 miles

Total mileage: 330 miles + 300 miles = 630 miles

50,132 + 630 = 50,762

88 Distance travelled in the UK: 55 miles × 2 = 110 miles

Distance travelled in France: (279km × 2) + 186km = 744km

5 miles = 8km; 1km = (5 ÷ 8) miles

744km = 744 × 5 ÷ 8 miles = 465 miles

Ratio of UK travel to French travel = 110:465

Dividing both by 5, gives, in lowest terms, the ratio as 22:93

89 $(194\,°F − 32) × \dfrac{5}{9} = 90\,°C$

$(95\,°F − 32) × \dfrac{5}{9} = 35\,°C$

90°C − 35°C = 55°C

90 Fuel needed: 455 miles @ 35 mpg = $\dfrac{455}{35}$ gallons = 13 gallons

1 gallon = 4.55 litres

13 gallons = 13 × 4.55 litres = 59.15 litres

59.15 litres @ £1.32 per litre = 59.15 × £1.32 = £78.078 = £78 (to nearest pound)

91 Distance = 2 × 45 miles = 90 miles

Fuel needed: 90 miles @ 40 mpg = $\dfrac{90}{40}$ gallons = 2.25 gallons

1 litre = 0.2 gallons; 1 gallon = $\dfrac{1}{0.2}$ litres

2.25 gallons = 2.25 × $\dfrac{1}{0.2}$ litres = 11.25 litres

92   Mean distance = $\dfrac{65\text{km}}{25}$ = $\dfrac{65,000\text{m}}{25}$ = 2600m

93   Mean = $\dfrac{(24+36)}{2}$ = $\dfrac{60}{2}$ = 30   OR $\dfrac{24}{60}$ × 100% = 40%

30 out of 60 = $\dfrac{30}{60}$ = 50% $\dfrac{36}{60}$ × 100% = 60%

Mean: $\dfrac{40\%+60\%}{2}$ = 50%

94   Total marks: 34 + 46 + 67 + 76 + 23 + 98 + 67 + 56 + 57 + 66 + 34 + 67 + 39 + 89 + 45 + 67 + 99 + 67 + 43 + 56 + 77 = 1273

Number of results = 21

Mean = $\dfrac{1273}{21}$ = 60.619 = 61 (to the nearest whole number)

95   Total years: 6 × 11 = 66

Total months: 6 + 9 + 11 + 2 + 10 + 4 = 42

66 ÷ 6 = 11 years

42 ÷ 6 = 7 months

11 years 7 months

96   Week 4 in table: −3°C + −1°C + 1°C + 2°C + 3°C = 2°C

$\dfrac{2°C}{5}$ = 0.4°C

97   Test A: $\dfrac{13}{20}$ = 0.65

Test B: $\dfrac{16}{25}$ = 0.64

Test C: $\dfrac{22}{40}$ = 0.55

Test D: $\dfrac{19}{30}$ = 0.63

Average = $\dfrac{0.65+0.64+0.55+0.63}{4}$

= $\dfrac{2.47}{4}$ = 0.62 (2 dp)

98   £832.50/90 = £9.25

99   Total number of lengths = (5 × 10 lengths) + (6 × 11 lengths) + (7 × 12 lengths) + (4 × 13 lengths) + (3 × 14 lengths) = 50 lengths + 66 lengths + 84 lengths + 52 lengths + 42 lengths = 294 lengths

Total money = 294 lengths × £3.25/length = £955.50

100   Total score = 32 × 54% = 1728%

1728% + 21% = 1749%

Number of scores = 32 + 1 = 33

$$\frac{1749\%}{33} = 53\%$$

101   Interpreting the tally marks, the total number of pupils:

3 + 5 + 4 + 9 + 6 = 27

Middle pupil is number 14

3 + 5 + 4 = 12

The 14th pupil is in the next group

13 lengths

102   Middle pupil of 100: need to average data for pupils 50 and 51

24 + 42 = 66 > 50

Pupils 50 and 51 each have 1 sibling.

103   Number of pupils: 3 + 3 + 4 + 18 + 13 = 41 pupils.

Middle pupil is pupil number 21

3 + 3 + 4 = 10

3 + 3 + 4 + 18 = 28

21st pupil's distance is in the 4th group

Number of laps: 5

5 × 1700m = 8500m = 8.5km

104   Producing a tally chart:

12	|
13	|
14	|
15	|
16	|
18	|
19	|
22	||||
27	|||

22 occurs the most number of times

105   Interpreting the tally marks, the highest number of pupils (7) complete 12 lengths

106   The highest number of children (20) complete 6 laps; $6 \times 1700m = 10,200m = 10.2km$

107   Highest mark = 99; Lowest mark = 23; Range = $99 - 23 = 76$

108   2012: $86.3 - 45.6 = 40.7$

109   2013: $85.4 - 48.9 = 36.5$

2014: $79.1 - 50.2 = 28.9$

$36.5 - 28.9 = 7.6$

110   Actual age range = 8 months

Reading age range = 30 months

$30 - 8 = 22$ months

111   Temperatures in week 2, in order:

$-4°C; -3°C; -2°C; 2°C; 3°C$

Median is middle value: $-2°C$

112   Lowest temperature recorded = $-4°C$

Highest temperature recorded = $4°C$

Range is $8°C$

113

	Mon	Tue	Wed	Thu	Fri	Sum of temperatures
Week 1	−1	0	1	2	4	$-1 + 1 + 2 + 4 = 6$
Week 2	3	2	−4	−3	−2	$3 + 2 + -4 + -3 + -2 = -4$
Week 3	2	2	1	0	0	$2 + 2 + 1 = 5$
Week 4	−3	−1	1	2	3	$-3 + -1 + 1 + 2 + 3 = 2$
Week 5	4	0	0	−1	−4	$4 + -1 + -4 = -1$

All the samples are the same size, so you only need to add. Dividing by 5 for each one is unnecessary.

114   Mean percentage in 2013: $(61.9 + 75.4 + 48.9 + 58.4 + 85.4)/5 = 330/5 = 66$

Median percentage: 61.9

Difference: $66 - 61.9 = 4.1$

115   Statement A:

Week 1 mean in $°C = (-4 + -3 + -1 + 0 + 0)/5 = -8/5 = -1.6$

Week 1 median in $°C = -1$

Statement A is true.

Statement B:

Range: −4 °C to +5 °C = 9 °C

Statement B is not true.

Statement C:

°C	−4	−3	−2	−1	0
freq	1	2	1	2	3

°C	1	2	3	4	5
freq	0	3	0	2	1

Modes at 0 °C and 2 °C: bimodal

Statement C is true.

Statement D:

Week 2 mean in °C = (4 + 2 + −1 + −3 + −2)/5 = 0

Statement D is true.

116 Mean: (94.2 + 86.1 + 92.5 + 110.4 + 108.3 + 97.1) secs ÷ 6 = 588.6 secs ÷ 6 = 98.1 secs

Median: 6 data items; median is mean of third and fourth items when in order

(94.2 + 97.1) secs ÷ 2 = 95.65 secs

Difference: 98.1 secs − 95.65 secs = 2.45 secs

117 Statement A: Set 2 did better at the test than Set 4.

The highest test score for Set 2 exceeds that for Set 4 (93 > 85) but the median is lower (42 < 51) and the lowest score is also lower (11 < 15).

Statement A is not true.

Statement B: The range of marks was greater for Set 2 than for Set 4.

Range for Set 2 = 93 − 11 = 82

Range for Set 4 = 85 − 15 = 70

82 > 70

Statement B is true.

Statement C: At least half of all the pupils taking the test scored 43 or more.

Half of Set 2 scored 43 or more. Half of Set 4 scored 52 or more.

Statement C is true.

118 Statement A: All values are different so there is no modal value.

Statement A is true.

Statement B: Mean = sum of values ÷ number of values

$$= \frac{(85.0 + 78.7 + 75.1 + 66.3 + 87.5 + 92.2 + 102.0 + 101.2)\text{secs}}{8}$$

$$= \frac{688\,\text{secs}}{8} = 86 \text{ secs}$$

Statement B is not true.

Statement C:

Putting the times in order, the median is the mean of the fourth and fifth data items.

$$= \frac{(85.0 + 87.5)\text{ seconds}}{2}$$

= 86.25 seconds

Statement C is not true.

Statement D:

Pupil 4's time = 66.3 seconds

Next fastest pupil's time = 75.1 seconds

Difference = (75.1 − 66.3) seconds = 8.8 seconds = 9 seconds to the nearest second

Statement D is true.

119   Statement A: The mean attendance on Mondays is 3 higher than the mean attendance on Fridays.

Monday: 28 + 25 + 28 + 22 + 28 = 131

131/5 = 26.2

Friday: 25 + 24 + 21 + 26 + 20 = 116

116/5 = 23.2

Statement A is true.

Statement B: The range of attendance is 7.

Range is 28 − 20 = 8

Statement B is not true.

Statement C: The modal attendance in week 1 is 27.

Mode for week 1 is 27 (occurs twice)

Statement C is true.

120   Looking for data which shows the temperature staying the same or dropping:

In Week 1, the temperature dropped on Tuesday

In Week 2, it stayed the same on Tuesday

In Week 4, it stayed the same on Thursday

In Week 5, it dropped on Tuesday

Only in Week 3 did the temperature rise every day.

121 Selecting data from the PE row:

0.15 × 5 hours × 60 minutes/hour = 45 minutes

122 Mean running time = total time ÷ 5

Total time (in secs) = 94.2 + 86.1 + 92.5 + 110.4 + 108.3 = 491.5

491.5 secs ÷ 5 = 98.3 secs

Three of the 5 children were below this time: A, B and C

3 out of 5 = $\dfrac{3}{5}$ = 0.6

123 Difference = 0.62 − 0.44 = 0.18 = $\dfrac{18}{100}$ = $\dfrac{9}{50}$

124 2012 mean: $\dfrac{(62.5 + 72.8 + 45.6 + 59.6 + 86.3)}{5}$ = $\dfrac{326.8}{5}$ = 65.36

2014 mean: $\dfrac{59.6 + 76.9 + 50.2 + 57.9 + 79.1}{5}$ = $\dfrac{323.7}{5}$ = 64.74

Difference in the means: 65.36 − 64.74 = 0.6

125 Total fat: 0.5 + 0.3 + 0.65 + 0.25 = 1.7

Mean fat: $\dfrac{1.7}{4}$ = 0.425 = $\dfrac{425}{1000}$ = $\dfrac{17}{40}$

126

Portfolios	Selected
0–6	1
7–12	2
13–18	3

Pass	Merit	Distinction
3	2	1
2	3	2
2	1	2

Total of entries = 18

127 Pupil C: 35 − 39 = −4; Pupil D: 23 − 22 = +1; Pupil E: 56 − 44 = +12

128 Looking at English: 2 + 9 + 28 + 7 = 46

46 in the year group

Looking at science: 46 − 6 − 20 − 8 = 12

Number of pupils predicted level 3 science = 12

Below level 5: 6 + 12 + 20 = 38

38 out of 46 = $\dfrac{38}{46} = \dfrac{19}{23}$

129   2012 % of total = $\dfrac{4}{18} \times 100\% = 22\%$

2013: level 5 total is 25% = 12 ÷ 2 = 6

2013 level 3 % of total = 100 − (50 + 25) = 25

2014: 50% = 7 + 9 = 16

130   Year 4: 8–7 − 8–1 = 0–6; Year 6: 10–5 − 10–2 = 0–3; 6 + 5 + 3 = 14

$\dfrac{14 \text{ months}}{3}$ = 5 months (to the nearest whole number)

131   Total number of pupils in the school: 16 + 18 + 22 + 17 + 19 + 25 + 19 = 136

Total number of pupils living in the school village:
7 + 10 + 12 + 13 + 11 + 18 + 14 = 85

Percentage: 85 out of 136 = 85/136 × 100% = 63% to the nearest whole %

132   Rather than work out all the percentages, make an estimate of the highest proportion. Look at the smallest differences between the two sets of numbers.

Class	Proportion	%
R	$\dfrac{7}{16}$	
1	$\dfrac{10}{18}$	
2	$\dfrac{12}{22}$	
3	$\dfrac{13}{17}$	76.5
4	$\dfrac{11}{19}$	
5	$\dfrac{18}{25}$	72.0
6	$\dfrac{14}{19}$	73.6

Answer: (Year 3) 76.5%

133 2012: $\dfrac{4}{6+8+4} = \dfrac{4}{18} = 0.21$

2013: $\dfrac{6}{6+12+6} = \dfrac{6}{24} = 0.25$

2014: $\dfrac{6}{3+15+6} = \dfrac{6}{24} = 0.25$

0.25 > 0.24

Make sure only data for level 5 is used to arrive at the answer.

134 8 out of 6 + 8 + 4 = $\dfrac{8}{18}$

$\dfrac{8}{18} \times 100\% = 44.4\% = 44\%$ to the nearest whole number

135 Total number achieving level 4 and above = 12 + 13 + 16 + 8 + 2 + 4 + 0 + 0 + 1 = 56

Total number in Year 6 = 56 + 2 + 4 + 0 + 7 + 7 + 6 = 82

56 out of 82 = $\dfrac{56}{82} \times 100\% = 68.29\% = 68\%$ (to the nearest whole number)

136 Class (1): Total number in class = 2 + 7 + 12 + 8 + 0 = 29

Level 3 percentage = $\dfrac{7}{29} \times 100\% = 24\%$

Class (2): Total number in class = 4 + 7 + 13 + 2 + 0 = 26

Level 3 percentage = $\dfrac{7}{26} \times 100\% = 27\%$

Class (3): Total number in class = 0 + 6 + 16 + 4 + 1 = 27

Level 3 percentage = $\dfrac{6}{27} \times 100\% = 22\%$

137 211 − 57 − 46 − 34 = 74

211 − 42 − 79 − 41 = 49

42 + 79 = 121; $\dfrac{121}{211} \times 100\% = 57\%$

45 + 88 + 56 = 189; $\dfrac{189}{211} \times 100\% = 89.57\% = 90\%$

211 − 40 = 171; $\dfrac{171}{211} \times 100\% = 81\%$

138 0.63 + 0.06 = 0.69

It's not an increase by 6% but an increase by 6 percentage points.

0.69 × 211 = 146 (to the nearest whole number)

Pupils who this year gained A*–C: 45 + 88 = 133

Number of additional pupils = 146 − 133 = 13

139

Months	Diff. Autumn	Diff. Summer	Change
A	18	20	2
B	0	−2	−2
C	−2	−2	0
D	−2	−7	−5
E	−2	−8	−6
F	−8	−10	−2
G	1	0	−1
H	−11	−11	0

140 Statement A: The highest total amount of money raised was at the school fete.

Sponsored activities total:

£89.45 + £93.87 + £145.35 = £328.67

School fete total:

£167.22 + £75.50 + £105.43 = £348.15

Sales total:

£67.50 + £35.20 + £68.30 = £171

£348.15 > £328.67 > £171

Statement A is true.

Statement B: Charity A will receive £509 to the nearest whole £.

£328.67 + £348.15 + £171 = £847.82

£847.82 × 3/5 = £508.692 = £509 to the nearest whole £

Statement B is true.

Statement C: The median amount raised of all the items listed is £89.45.

Nine items: median is the fifth when listed in order

£35.20; £67.50; £68.30; £75.50; £89.45

Statement C is true.

141 Boys: $\dfrac{(76.4 + 79.6 + 75.8 + 78.5)}{4}$ = 310.3/4 = 77.575

Girls: $\dfrac{(75.3 + 78.7 + 78.3 + 78.7)}{4}$ = 77.75

Difference: 77.75 − 77.575 = 0.175 = 0.2 (to 1 dp)

Keep all the decimal places until the last stage of the calculation.

142 Statement A: The performance of the boys in the school is consistently below the national average.

The data for 2011 and 2012 contradict this statement.

Statement A is not true.

Statement B: The percentage of girls in the school achieving level 2 and above has increased every year.

The data for girls for 2011–2014 confirms this statement.

Statement B is true.

Statement C: The girls in the school consistently outperform the boys.

The data for girls, compared with that for the boys, confirms this statement.

Statement C is true.

Statement D: In 2013, the boys in the school were performing at 2.5% below the national average for that year.

2013 data for boys: 75.8 versus 78.3

78.3 − 75.8 = 2.5

Statement D is true.

143 78.5 + 0.6 = 79.1

78.7 + 0.2 = 78.9

89.2 + 0.6 = 89.8

87.4 + 0.2 = 87.6

144 Improvement is the difference between the before and after scores. Pupil F has the highest improvement.

	Before	After	Improvement
A	15	22	7
B	20	25	5
C	32	34	2
D	16	19	3
E	25	21	−4
F	20	32	12
G	16	19	3

	Before	After	Improvement
H	17	28	11
I	29	33	4
J	31	38	7

145   Statement A: All the boys achieved improved scores after the additional support.

The scores in the second column of the boys' table are all higher.

Statement A is true.

Statement B: 20% of the girls achieved a lower score after the additional support.

There are 5 girls. 20% is one girl. Girl E did score lower after support.

Statement B is true.

Statement C: The mean difference in the boys' scores before and after the additional support was 7.4.

Mean 'before' = (20 + 16 + 17 + 29 + 31)/5 = 22.6

Mean 'after' = (32 + 19 + 28 + 33 + 38)/5 = 30

Difference 30 − 22.6 = 7.4

Statement C is true.

Statement D: The median girls' score after the additional support was 25 marks.

Marks in order are: 19, 21, 22, 25, 34. 5 scores. Median is third: 22

Statement D is not true.

Statement E: Pupil G scored 47.5% in the task after additional support.

$19/40 \times 100\% = 47.5\%$

Statement E is true.

146   Statement A: Approximately $\frac{1}{10}$ of the pupils who took GCSE mathematics and GCSE music gained grades A* or A in both subjects.

Pupils who took GCSE mathematics and GCSE music and gained grades A* or A in both subjects = 5

Total number of students = 5 + 6 + 2 + 0 + 4 + 7 + 3 + 1 + 3 + 4 + 5 + 2 + 0 + 1 + 1 + 7 = 51

$$\frac{5}{51} \cong \frac{1}{10}$$

Statement A is true.

Statement B: More than ⅙ of the pupils taking both GCSE mathematics and GCSE music gained grades F or G in mathematics.

Number gaining F/G in mathematics = 0 + 1 + 1 + 7 = 9

Number taking both = 51 as above

$$\frac{9}{51} = \frac{3}{17} > \frac{1}{6} = \frac{3}{18}$$

Statement B is true.

Statement C: $\frac{3}{4}$ of the pupils who gained C and above in mathematics, gained A or A* in music.

Number who gained C or above in mathematics = 5 + 6 + 2 + 0 + 4 + 7 + 3 + 1 = 28

Of these, number who gained A*/A in music = 5 + 4 = 9

9 out of 28 = $\frac{9}{28} \neq \frac{3}{4}$

Statement C is not true.

147 From mathematics/French table, number gaining E and above:

5 + 8 + 1 + 2 + 11 + 5 + 3 + 9 + 11 = 55

Total number of pupils = 11 + 29 + 19 + 26 = 85

Fraction = $\frac{55}{85} = \frac{11}{17}$

Give answers in the lowest terms.

148 From mathematics/music table, number of pupils achieving C and above in both GCSE music and in GCSE mathematics = 3 + 2 + 1 + 9 = 15

Total number of pupils = 4 + 15 + 10 + 2 = 31

Proportion = 15/31 = 0.48 = 0.5 (to 1 dp)

149 Statement A: More than 40% of pupils in Years 7 and 8 have school dinners.

Total number of pupils = 54 + 114 + 102 = 270

40% of 270 = 108

114 > 108

Statement A is true.

Statement B: One-fifth of the pupils make other arrangements.

$$\frac{54}{270} = \frac{1}{5}$$

Statement B is true.

Statement C: Less than 1 in 3 pupils has a packed lunch.

$\dfrac{1}{3}$ of 270 = 90; 102 > 90

Statement C is not true.

150   Total number of pupils = 54 + 114 + 102 = 270

114 + 24 = 138

138 out of 270 = $\dfrac{138}{270} \times 100\%$ = 51.1% =

51% (to nearest whole number)

151   100 − 15 − 26 − 36 − 22 = 1

1% spend more than 20 hours

1% of 74 = 0.01 × 74 = 0.74 = 1 (to the nearest whole person!)

152   26% of 74 pupils = 0.26 × 74 pupils = 19 pupils

Add 3 pupils: now 22 pupils playing 11–15 hours and 77 pupils in total.

% playing games for 11–15 hours per week is 22 ÷ 77 × 100 = 29 (A)

NB: not B because must still add up to 100%

153   In Year 7, 'None' occupies ¼ of the pie: 25%

In Year 7, 'Chess' occupies the same proportion as 'Music': 15%

In Year 7, 'Film' = 100 − 25 − 15 − 25 − 15 = 20

In Year 10, 'Film' = 100 − 30 − 10 − 35 − 5 = 20

154   School A: 45% of 103 = 0.45 × 103 = 46.35

School B: 25% of 95 = 0.25 × 95 = 23.75

46.35 + 23.75 = 70.1 = 70 (to the nearest whole number)

155   Statement A: A greater proportion of pupils are taking A levels at school B than at school A.

The sectors show percentages, so direct comparison of the sizes of the sectors can be made. The sector for A levels is larger in school A's pie.

Statement A is not true.

Statement B: One-quarter of the pupils at school A are planning on taking other vocational programmes.

School A's pie shows 'other vocational programmes as 25%'; 25% = $\dfrac{1}{4}$.

Statement B is true.

Statement C: More than half the pupils at school B are planning on doing an apprenticeship.

Apprenticeship sector in school B's pie chart shows 60%; 60% > 50% = $\frac{1}{2}$.

Statement C is true.

156 Statement A: The proportion of pupils achieving A*–A improved in year two.

A*–A sector is smaller in year two chart.

Statement A is not true.

Statement B: The proportion of D–G grades remained the same.

The D–G sector is smaller in year two chart.

Statement 2 is not true.

Statement C: The proportion of pupils achieving A*–C grades improved in year two.

The D–G sector is smaller in year two chart, so combined other grades increased in year two.

Statement C is true.

Statement D: We are not able to tell whether more pupils achieved a C and above in year two.

The pie charts show proportions only so it is not possible to say how many pupils achieved each grade.

Statement D is true.

157 From the pie chart, in year one, half the pupils achieved grades D–G.

$\frac{130 \text{ pupils}}{2}$ = 65 pupils

In year two, 30% of 120 gained grades D–G.

30% of 120 pupils = 0.3 × 120 pupils = 36 pupils

Comparing: 65 pupils − 36 pupils = 29 pupils

158 Largest sector for level 5 is on the chart for 2011.

159 Combining the sectors for level 4 and 5, in 2012 they form half of the circle.

160 Data for level 4 and above:

A: 30 + 36 = 66; B: 50 + 20 = 70; C: 62 + 14 = 76; D = 70 + 5 = 75:

In order: 66, 70, 75, 76

Median = $\frac{(70 + 75)}{2}$ = 72.5

161 $\frac{40}{75}$ × 100% = 53%, ie A

162 Statement A: The mean percentage of GCSE grades A*–C for the first four years of the chart was 44% (to the nearest whole number).

Mean for years 2008–2011: (35% + 42% + 47% + 51%)/4 = 43.75% = 44% (to nearest whole number)

Statement A is true.

Statement B: The percentage of GCSE grades A*–C in 2008 was less than half of that in 2014.

2008 = 35%; 2014 = 75%

35 ÷ 75 = 0.46 < 0.5

Statement B is true.

Statement C: The percentage of grades A*–C increased each year.

2013 saw a decrease.

Statement C is not true.

Statement D: The median percentage of GCSE grades A*–C over the seven-year period was 51%.

The middlemost value if the columns are arranged in order of height is the data for 2011, so the median value was 51%.

Statement D is true.

163 Multiplying each value by its frequency, the total number of days of unauthorised absence

= 15 × 1 + 12 × 2 + 8 × 3 + 4 × 4 + 18 × 5 + 7 × 6 + 5 × 7 + 4 × 8 + 7 × 9 + 15 × 10

= 15 + 24 + 24 + 16 + 90 + 42 + 35 + 32 + 63 + 150

= 491

164 Statement A: The range of days of unauthorised absence is 10.

The highest number of days of consecutive unauthorised absence is 10; the lowest is 1.

Range = 10 – 1 = 9

Statement A is not true.

Statement B: The highest frequency (tallest bar) is for 5 consecutive days of unauthorised days of absence; the mode is 5.

Statement B is true.

Statement C: The median number of consecutive days of unauthorised absence is 5.5.

Accumulating the frequencies:

1	15	15
2	12	27
3	8	35
4	4	39
5	**18**	**57**
6	7	64
7	5	69
8	4	73
9	7	80
10	15	95

95 recorded absences; median is the 48th

39 < 48 < 57 so median is 5

Statement C is not true.

165 Increases:

2008: 10 − 10 = 0

2009: 15 − 10 = 5

2010: 18 − 15 = 3

2011: 20 − 18 = 2

2012: 23 − 20 = 3

2013: 25 − 23 = 2

2014: 29 − 25 = 4

166 Average = $\dfrac{(10 + 10 + 15 + 18 + 20 + 23 + 25 + 29)}{8} = \dfrac{150}{8} = 18.758$ years of data

167 Median = average of data items 4 and 5

2010: 18

2011: 20

$\dfrac{(18 + 20)}{2} = \dfrac{38}{2} = 19$

168 Reading the column heights:

15 + 35 + 12 = 62

Proportion = $\dfrac{62}{104} = 0.5961 \ldots = 0.6$ (to 1 dp)

169   Data from chart (first and third columns) = 15 + 12 = 27

Plus additional 25: 27 + 25 = 52

Proportion: 52 out of 104 = $\dfrac{52}{104} \times 100\% = 50\%$

170   Statement A: The overall results in test 2 were higher than in test 1.

Test 2 shows generally higher marks: more achieved marks of between 61 and 80 for test 2. Fewer achieved marks of between 0 and 60 for test 2.

Statement A is true.

Statement B: The scores between 41 and 60 decreased in test 2 by one-third.

$\dfrac{3}{9} = \dfrac{1}{4}$

Statement B is true.

Statement C: 85% of pupils scored more than 40% in test 2.

6 + 15 + 3 = 24

$\dfrac{24}{30} = 80\%$

Statement C is not true.

171   Statement A: In all four years, the proportion of girls applying to university is greater than the proportion of boys applying for university.

%	2011	2012	2013	2014
Girls	30	40	24	30
Boys	25	25	26	35

In 2013 and 2014, the percentage of girls is less than that of boys.

Statement A is not true.

Statement B: The highest proportion of boys applying for university was in 2012.

In 2014, 35% applied, which is greater than the 25% in 2012.

Statement B is not true.

Statement C: The highest proportion of all students applying for university was in 2012.

For both 2012 and 2014 the percentage is 65%.

Statement C is not true.

Statement D: In each year, more than 50% of the students applied for university.

Totals are:

%	2011	2012	2013	2014
Girls	30	40	24	30
Boys	25	25	26	35
Total	55	65	50	65

In 2013 only 50% applied.

Statement D is true.

172 $\dfrac{19}{40} + \dfrac{29}{40} + \dfrac{27}{40} = \dfrac{75}{40}$

Mean $= \dfrac{75}{40} \div 3 = \dfrac{25}{40} = 0.625 \times 1005 = 62.5\% =$

63% (to nearest whole number)

173   Statement A: The mean mark for test 1 is 25.

Test 1 results in order: 19, 25, 25, 27, 36.

Median is third value = 25.

Mode = 25 (frequency 2)

Mean $= \dfrac{(25 + 36 + 27 + 25 + 19)}{5} = 26.4$

Statement A is not true.

Statement B: The range of marks in test 3 is 17.

Highest = 24; lowest = 15; range = 24 − 15 = 9

Statement B is true.

Statement C: The lowest mark was achieved in test 1.

The lowest mark was 15, pupil E in test 3.

Considering the total marks achieved:

Test 1: 25 + 36 + 27 + 25 + 19 = 132

Test 2: 28 + 31 + 29 + 27 + 18 = 133

Test 3: 16 + 24 + 19 + 22 + 15 = 96

Statement C is not true.

Statement D: The modal mark over all three tests was 25.

There are three modes: 19, 25 and 27.

Statement D is not true.

174 Data for 'Resistant materials' is

Year one: 35%

Year five: 10%

Drop in popularity = 35% − 10% = 25%

175 Data is: 40 30 50 35 25

In order: 25 30 35 40 50

Middle value is 35

176 Column 4 has the right data in the right order according to the legend.

177 55 + 20 + 35 = 110

Mean = $\dfrac{110}{3}$ = 36.666 = 37% to the nearest whole percentage

178 Statement A: In school 3, 65% were graded as 'Needs improvement'.

Reading the school 3 column, 35% (values between 65% and 100%) were graded 'needs improvement'.

Statement A is not true.

Statement B: More than half the lessons in school 1 were graded 'Needs improvement'.

Reading the school 1 column, 55% were graded 'needs improvement' (between 45% and 100%).

55% > 50% = $\dfrac{1}{2}$

Statement B is true.

Statement C: In school 2, $\dfrac{4}{5}$ of the lessons were graded 'good' or 'outstanding'.

Reading the school 2 column, 80% were graded 'good' or 'outstanding': 80% = $\dfrac{4}{5}$

Statement C is true.

179 School 2: 5 lessons are outstanding

On bar chart shown as 25%

1 lesson represents 25% ÷ 5 = 5%

100% ÷ 5% = 20%

180 The section within the bar needs to show the accumulation of the data:

15

15 + 75 = 90

90 + 10 = 100

181 Examine the points near the top right-hand corner.

182 The number of points in the top right-hand quadrant = 9

The total number of points = 20

$\dfrac{9}{20}$ = 0.45

183 The school data exceeds the national data when the graph is higher, ie in 2011.

184 Statement A: The school's highest percentage score was in 2011.

The 2013 percentage score is higher than the 2011 percentage score.

Statement A is not true.

Statement B: 2010 was the year when the school made the greatest amount of improvement in percentage points.

Data is:

Year	% score	Change
2008	60	
2009	60	0
2010	73	13
2011	79	6
2012	73.5	−4.5
2013	86	12.5

Statement B is true.

Statement C: The percentage of pupils gaining 5 A*–C grades in the school fell in 2012.

Data table above shows negative change in 2012.

Statement C is true.

Statement D: The school is performing consistently below the national average.

The school performs higher than the national average in 2011.

Statement D is not true.

185 Cost = £300 + 100 × £1 = £400

186 Reading the graph at 30 miles the values are:

Dashed: £150

Dotty: £275

Difference = £275 − £150 = £125

187 Statement A: For a distance of 20 miles, the Dotty Company charges £125 more than the Dashed Company.

Distance of 20 miles:

Reading up from 20 miles on the horizontal axis, Dotty charges £250, Dashed charges £100

£250 − £100 = £150

Statement A is not true.

Statement B: Both companies charge the same amount for a distance of 80 miles.

At 80 miles, the lines meet, indicating the same price for the same distance.

Statement B is true.

Statement C: The cost of hiring the Dashed Company for a journey of 120 miles is £600.

Dashed charges are rising by £100 for every 20 miles.

For 100 miles, the charge is £500.

For 120 miles: £500 + £100 = £600

Statement C is true.

Statement D: The Dotty Company is cheaper for all journeys up to 60 miles.

The dashed line is below the dotty line for 0–60 miles, so the Dashed Company is cheaper for those distances.

Statement D is not true.

188 $124 - 48 = 76$

189   Statement A: Altogether, 126 pupils took part in the survey.

The grid divisions are 4 (20 ÷ 5) on the vertical scale. The highest point, which shows the total number of pupils, is at 124.

Statement A is not true.

Statement B: Half the pupils did less than 15 hours per week.

Half the pupils = 62

Reading across from 62 on the vertical axis, and down onto the horizontal axis, the reading is less than 15.

Statement B is true.

Statement C: Approximately 48 pupils did less than 10 hours per week.

Reading across from the vertical axis at 48, and then down to the horizontal axis, the reading is 10. This means 48 pupils did less than 10 hours homework.

Statement C is true.

Statement D: Exactly 12 pupils did more than 20 hours per week.

Read up from the horizontal axis at 20 hours, and across to the vertical axis, the reading is 115 pupils.

$124 - 115 = 9$

Statement D is not true.

190   Inspection of the boxplots to match the data

Data is:

	Low	LQ	M	UQ	High
A	20	45	60	90	95
B	10	30	50	75	90
C	45	60	64	80	90
D	20	35	50	65	80

191 $\frac{1}{4}$ scored between 50 and 80

$\frac{1}{4}$ of 48 pupils = 12 pupils

192   Statement A: Many pupils found test 2 easier than test 1.

The marks for test 2 are generally lower, implying that it was more difficult.

Statement A is not true.

Statement B: The interquartile range of test 1 is more than twice that of the interquartile range of test 2.

Test 1 interquartile range 80 − 25 = 55

Test 2 interquartile range 45 − 20 = 25

55 > 25 × 2

Statement B is true.

Statement C: The range of marks for test 2 is 60.

Range for test 2 is 60 − 5 = 55

Statement C is not true.

Statement D: 25% of the pupils gained 80% or more in test 1.

Upper quartile for test 1 is 80%; above that 25% gained higher marks.

Statement D is true.

193   An increase by 13 percentage points increases all the marks, so the interquartile range is not changed.

45 − 20 = 25

194   Class 1: 80 − 20 = 60

Class 2: 85 − 30 = 55

Difference: 60 − 55 = 5

195 The interquartile range will remain the same, since all marks have been reduced: 70 − 45 = 25.

196 Statement A: The range of marks for class B is lower than for class A.

It is possible to decide on the size of the ranges by inspection. It can also be 'proved' mathematically:

Class A range: 98 − 44 = 54

Class B range: 75 − 45 = 30

Statement A is true.

Statement B: Fewer people in class A gained over 76% than in class B.

76% is the upper quartile for test A, and the highest mark for test B. 25% of pupils scored above 76 in test A and none scored higher in test B.

Statement B is not true.

Statement C: 21 pupils in class B scored 60 or more in the test.

60 is the lower quartile for test B.

75% of the pupils = $\frac{3}{4} \times 28 = 21$

Statement C is true.

Statement D: Seven pupils in class A gained more than 80%.

$\frac{7}{28} = 25$.

The upper quartile is marked at a score of less than 80%.

Statement D is not true.

197 By inspection, the values for boxplot 2 match.

	Low	LQ	M	UQ	High
1	30	45	60	75	80
2	**30**	**50**	**70**	**80**	**85**
3	30	38	50	70	90
4	30	40	65	75	85

198 Year four median = 42

Year five median = 48

Increase = 48 − 42 = 6

199 Year five: 59 − 35 = 24

Year four: 49 − 32 = 17

24 − 17 = 7

200 Statement A: The median has increased by 16 points over the three-year period.

Median in year three is 36; median in year five is 48

Increase is 12

Statement A is not true.

Statement B: There is a greater range of scores in year five than in either of the other two years.

Distance from top to bottom is greater for year five.

Statement B is true.

Statement C: The interquartile range in year four is 17.

Interquartile range in year three is 43 − 25 = 18

Statement C is true.

Statement D: All pupils have improved in reading over the three-year period.

It is not possible to tell whether all the pupils improved, as the boxplot only provides a summary of results.

Statement D is not true.

201 Look for the boxplot showing the highest top mark, and the highest bottom mark.

202 n = 104

$$\frac{n}{10} = \frac{104}{10} = 10.4$$

10.4 + 7 = 17.4 = 17 (to the nearest whole number)

203 F − 32 = 75 − 32 = 43

$$C = 5 \times \frac{43}{9} = 24$$

75°F = 24°C

204 65 × 0.6 + Part two mark × 0.4 = 70

39 + Part two mark × 0.4 = 70

Part two mark × 0.4 = 31

Part two mark = 31/0.4 = 78

205 $\frac{18}{45} \times 0.4 + \frac{28}{60} \times 0.6 = 0.16 + 0.28 = 0.44 = 0.44 \times 100\% = 44\%$

206 Paper 1:

30% of 63 out of 80 as a % = $0.3 \times \frac{63}{80} \times 100\% = 23.6\%$

Paper 2:

70% of 49 out of 65 as a % = $0.7 \times \dfrac{49}{65} \times 100\% = 52.8\%$

207   First paper: $\dfrac{16}{40} \times 100\% = 40\%$

20% of 40% = $\dfrac{20}{100} \times 40\% = 8\%$

Second paper: $\dfrac{45}{80} \times 100\% = 56.25\%$

80% of 56.25% = $\dfrac{80}{100} \times 56.25\% = 45\%$

Final score: 8% + 45% = 53%

208 $(0.3 \times 105 + 0.5 \times 96 + 0.2 \times 125)/2.5 = (31.5 + 48 + 25)/2.5 = 104.5/2.5$
= 41.8 = 42 (to the nearest whole number)

209   Time = distance ÷ speed

125 miles ÷ 50mph = 2.5 hours

11:00 − 2.5 hours = 8:30

210   Time taken to walk = 12km ÷ 5kph = 2.4 hours

0.4 of an hour is 24 minutes (0.4 × 60)

2 × 15 minutes = 30 minutes of breaks.

Total time = 2 hours 54 minutes

09:00 + 2:54 = 11:54

Finishing time = 11:54

211   11:15 + 0:30 = 11:45: time of leaving Calais: 11:45

48km × 5 ÷ 8 = 30 miles

30 miles ÷ 45mph = $\dfrac{2}{3}$ hour = 40 minutes

11:45 + 0:40 = 12:25

Time at hotel: 12:25

212   5 miles = 8km; 1km = $\dfrac{5}{8}$ miles

120km = $120 \times \dfrac{5}{8}$ miles = 75 miles

Time: 75 miles @ 50 mph takes $\dfrac{75}{50}$ hours = 1.5 hours

16:30 − 1.5 hours = 15:00

Leave at 15:00

Numeracy practice paper 1

Mental arithmetic questions

1 20×10 minutes = 200 minutes

200 + 15 = 215

$215 \div 60$ = 3 hours and some left over!

$60 \times 3 = 180$

215 − 180 = 35

2 $£\dfrac{253.05}{3} = £84.35$

3 $24 \times 2.5 = £60$

4 $1.2\text{km} \times 4 = 4.8\text{km}$

5 $\dfrac{65}{100} \times 80 = 13 \times 4 = 52$

6   €360 = $360 \times £0.8 = £288$

7 $\dfrac{716}{10} \times 1074 = 2 \times 358 = 716$

$\dfrac{716}{10}$ = 72 (rounded up to the next whole number)

8 $3 \times 2\text{km} = 6\text{km}$

Time = distance/speed

$\dfrac{6\text{km}}{8\text{kph}} = \dfrac{3}{4}$ hr = 45 mins

9 $\dfrac{80}{100} \times 240 = 8 \times 24 = 192$

10 $0.4 \times 7.3 = \dfrac{(4 \times 73)}{100} = \dfrac{292}{100} = 2.92$

11 $\dfrac{51}{60} \times 100\% = 17 \times 5\% = 85\%$

12 $6 \times 25 = 150$

$\dfrac{150}{40}$ = 4 packs (rounded up to the nearest whole number)

Onscreen questions

1 Number of siblings:

$(0 \times 5) + (1 \times 8) + (2 \times 7) + (3 \times 6) + (4 \times 3) + (5 \times 1) = 0 + 8 + 14 + 18 + 12 + 5 = 57$

Number of children surveyed:

$5 + 8 + 7 + 6 + 3 + 1 = 30$

Mean = $\dfrac{57}{30}$ = 1.9

2 Number of staff = $6 + 9 + 5 + 8 + 7 + 1 = 36$

Number who cycle = $5 + 1 = 6$

Percentage who cycle = $\dfrac{6}{36} \times 100\% = 16.6666\% = 16.67\%$ (to 2 dp)

3 Counting the number of points above the diagonal, there are 11 pupils who did better in the oral test.

$\dfrac{11}{28} = 0.3928 = 0.4$ (to 1 dp)

4 Mon. wk 1

$127 - 25 - 24 - 22 - 28 = 28$

Tue. wk 5

$126 - 26 - 26 - 27 - 24 = 23$

Wed. wk 2

$130 - 27 - 27 - 28 - 22 = 26$

Fri. wk 2

$121 - 25 - 21 - 26 - 25 = 24$

5 Goals scored in six games:

$6 \times 4.8 = 28.8$; she scored 29 goals in 6 games

$7 \times 5 = 35$

$35 - 29 = 6$

She must score 6 goals in the seventh game

6 Statement A: Test 3 has the smallest range of marks.

Visual inspection shows test 3 has the smallest range.

Looking at the data

Test	High	Low	Range
1	80	5	75
2	95	10	85
3	100	55	45
4	99	40	59

Statement A is true.

Statement B: Test 2 was found to be the most difficult.

Test 1's highest mark is lower than that of test 2, and test 1's lowest mark is lower than that of test 2, so test 2 is not the most difficult.

Statement B is not true.

Statement C: The interquartile range for test 1 was 40.

Test 1: LQ = 25; UQ = 65; IQR = 65 − 25 = 40

Statement C is true.

Statement D: Over half the pupils achieved over 65% in test 4.

The median value for test 4 is 65.

Statement D is true.

7 42 + 6 = 48

$\dfrac{48}{15}$ = 3 (rounded down to the nearest whole number)

This means there will be 3 free places

48 − 3 = 45

45 × £15.55 = £699.75

£699.75/48 = £14.58 (to the nearest penny)

£14.58 + £18 = £32.58

8 Total number of students = 46 + 89 + 27 + 18 = 180

English A*–C:

46 + 89 = 135

135/180 = 75%

New target = 81%

0.81 × 180 = 146 (rounded up to nearest whole number)

146 − 135 = 11

9 Total number of students = 46 + 89 + 27 + 18 = 180

% A*–A grades:

$\dfrac{46}{180}$ = 25.56%

$\dfrac{37}{180}$ = 20.56%

$\dfrac{42}{180}$ = 23.33%

$\dfrac{51}{180}$ = 28.33%

Mean percentage:

$$\frac{(25.55 + 20.55 + 23.33 + 28.33)\%}{4} = \frac{97.76\%}{4} = 24.44\% = 24\% \text{ (to nearest whole number)}$$

10 Statement A: There are more teachers under the age of 30 in the school in 2014 than in 2009.

The sector for 'Under 30' is smaller in the 2014 pie chart than in the 2009 pie chart.

Statement A is true.

Statement B: The age profile of the teachers in 2009 was generally younger than in 2014.

There were more under 30s and 30–39, but also more 50–59.

Statement B is not true.

Statement C: Approximately 75% of teachers in the school in 2009 were aged between 30 and 49 years.

In the 2009 chart, combining the 30–39 and 40–49 sectors creates a slice approximately 75% of the pie.

Statement C is true.

11

Pupil	High	Low	Range
1	65	52	13
2	60	47	13
3	61	57	14
4	56	32	24

12 Statement A: The mode and the median are the same.

Data in order: 39, 62, 65, 65, 74, 87

Median = 65

65 appears twice so mode = 65

Statement A is true

Statement B: The mean is lower than the median.

$$\text{Mean} = \frac{(39 + 62 + 65 + 65 + 74 + 87)}{6} = \frac{392}{6} = 65.3$$

65.3 > 65

Statement B is not true.

Statement C: The range is 48.

Range = 87 − 39 = 48

Statement C is true.

13   A: 14%; B: 6%; C: −14%; D: 1%; E: 12%. Pupil A made the most progress.

14   30 miles per hour means every mile takes 2 minutes

35 miles will take 70 minutes

Journey time = 1 hour 10 minutes

Play starts 19:30

Arrival time = 19:15

Departure time = 18:05

15   Car drivers: 8 + 6 = 14

Sample: 6 + 8 + 6 + 8 + 6 + 3 = 37

14/37 × 250 = 94.59 = 95 (to the next nearest whole number)

16   Median – there are 80 in the survey, so read across from 40 on the vertical axis, and then down to the horizontal axis.

18 hours.

Numeracy practice paper 2

Mental arithmetic questions

1 $\dfrac{80}{200} = \dfrac{8}{20} = \dfrac{4}{10} = 0.4$

2 $\dfrac{18}{25} \times 100\% = 18 \times 4\% = 72\%$

$\dfrac{18}{25} \times 100\% = 16 \times 5\% = 80\%$

$\dfrac{(72+80)\%}{2} = 76\%$

3 $\dfrac{33}{220} = \dfrac{3}{20}$

4   10% of £260 = £26

20% of £260 = £52

£260 + £52 = £312

5 $0.3 \times 5.7 = 3 \times \dfrac{57}{100} = \dfrac{171}{100} = 1.71$

6 $\dfrac{5m}{0.45m} = \dfrac{500}{45} = 11.11 = 11$ (rounded down to nearest whole number)

7 $44.31\% + 40.69\% = 85\% = \dfrac{85}{100} = \dfrac{17}{20}$

8   20 + 22 + 17 + 19 + 18 = 96

$\dfrac{96}{5}$ = 19.2

9   70% of 60 = 0.7 × 60 = 42

10   £160.50 × 33 = £5296.50

11   1 yen = £0.005; £1 = 1/0.005 yen

£150 = 150/0.005 yen = 30,000 yen

12   47 mins + 15 mins = 62 mins = 1 hr 2 mins

Lesson ends 11:00

Start film at 9:58

Onscreen questions

1   1 hr 30 mins + 1 hr 25 mins + 1 hr + 1 hr = 4 hrs 55 mins

5 × 4 hours = 20 hours

5 × 55 mins = 275 mins = 4 hrs 35 mins

20 hours + 4 hours + 35 mins = 24 hours 35 mins

2   Statement A: The average mark for test 5 was higher than any other test.

Total marks for each test are

259 (1), 257 (2), 260 (3), 277 (4) and 276 (5)

276 < 277

Statement A is not true.

Statement B: The greatest range of marks was achieved in test 2.

No need to calculate all the ranges.

Test 1 range = 94 − 38 = 56

Test 2 range = 89 − 34 = 55

56 > 55

Statement B is not true.

Statement C: The median mark for test 1 was 63.5.

Marks in order: 38, 43, 84, 94

Median: $\dfrac{(43+84)}{2}$ = 63.5 Statement C is true.

Statement D: Pupil A achieved the lowest mean score.

There is no need to calculate all the mean marks. Pupils B and C both achieved higher marks than A in every test, so their mean will be higher.

Pupil D mean = $\dfrac{(38+45+52+61+67)}{5} = \dfrac{263}{5}$ = 52.6

Pupil A mean = $\dfrac{(43+34+52+49+63)}{5} = \dfrac{241}{5} = 48.2$

Statement D is true.

3   Mean = $\dfrac{(49+87+80+61+58)}{5} = \dfrac{335}{5} = 67$

Median:

In order: 49, 58, 61, 80, 87

Median = 61

Difference = 67 − 61 = 6

4   Pupil A

$\dfrac{(45+2\times52+3+75)}{6}$

$= \dfrac{(45+104+225)}{6}$

$\dfrac{374}{6} = 62.33$

Pupil B

$\dfrac{(63+2\times61+3\times62)}{6}$

$= \dfrac{(63+122+186)}{6}$

$= \dfrac{371}{6} = 61.83$

Pupil C

$\dfrac{(82+2\times65+3\times61)}{6}$

$= \dfrac{(82+130+183)}{6}$

$= \dfrac{395}{6} = 65.83$

65.83 > 62.33 > 61.83

Pupil C scores highest

5   Statement A: The median mark for test 2 is higher than the median mark for test 1.

For median, compare score for 30th pupil.

Test 1 median < 60

Test 2 median = 60

Statement A is true.

Statement B: The interquartile range is higher in test 2 than in test 1.

IQR is between 15th and 45th pupils.

Test 1 IRQ = 64 − 44 = 20

Test 2 IRQ = 68 − 48 = 20

Statement B is not true.

Statement C: 25% of pupils in test 1 obtained less than 40 marks.

25% of 60 = 15

Test 1 for 40 marks: 12 pupils scored less than 40

Statement C is not true.

Statement D: The overall marks for test 2 are higher than for test 1.

The test 1 graph is above and left of the test 2 graph.

Statement D is true.

6   Total number of bikes checked = 12 + 15 + 22 + 14 + 9 + 2 + 1 = 75

Total number of faults =

$(0 \times 12) + (1 \times 15) + (2 \times 22) + (3 \times 14) + (4 \times 9) + (5 \times 2) + (6 \times 1)$

= 0 + 15 + 44 + 42 + 36 + 10 + 6

= 153

Mean = $\frac{153}{75}$ = 2.04 = 2 (to the nearest whole number)

7   Statement A: The percentage of pupils achieving level 4 and above has steadily increased over the last five years.

The level 4 and above graph dips in 2013.

Statement A is not true.

Statement B: The best results of the last five years were achieved in 2014.

The high point for level 4 and above is 2014. For level 5 and above, 2014 is the same as 2010 but higher than any other year.

Statement B is true.

Statement C: In 2011, 57% of pupils at Key Stage 2 achieved scores below level 4.

Data for 2011 shows 84% achieved level 4 or above.

100% − 87% = 13%

Statement C is not true.

Statement D: In 2010 and in 2014, half of all pupils achieved level 5 and above.

Data for 2010: 50%

Data for 2015: 50%

Statement D is true.

8 Pets:

$(0 \times 5) + (1 \times 9) + (2 \times 8) + (3 \times 4) + (4 \times 3) + (5 \times 2) + (6 \times 1)$

$= 0 + 9 + 16 + 12 + 12 + 10 + 6$

$= 65$

Children:

$5 + 9 + 8 + 4 + 3 + 2 + 1 = 32$

Mean $= \dfrac{65}{32} = 2.03125 = 2.03$

9 $3 + 4 = 7$

$\dfrac{£7054}{7} = £1007.71$

Retain decimal places (pence) until the final calculation.

$£1007.71 \times 4 = £4030.85 = £4031$ (to the nearest whole £)

10 Imagine a line starting at (50, 0) and ending at (100, 50) and identify the point on that line: (85, 35).

11 Transport: $\dfrac{£2352}{30} = £78.40$

Accommodation: $\dfrac{54,360\,\text{SEK}}{30} = 1812$ SEK

£1 = 12.08 SEK

1 SEK = £1/12.08

1812 SEK = $\dfrac{£1812}{12.08} = £150$

Food, etc: 1184 SEK = $\dfrac{£1184}{12.08} = £98.01$

Total: $£78.40 + £150 + £98.01 = £326.41$

12 $101 - 84 = 17$

$\dfrac{17}{115} \times 100\% = 14.78\% = 14.8\%$ (1 dp)

13 The percentages given are for different quantities, so it would be incorrect to add the three percentages together and divide by 3.

Total number of girls = 113 + 52 + 79 = 244

Total number of pupils in the three schools = 210 + 108 + 152 = 470

Percentage = $\dfrac{244}{470} \times 100\% = 51.9\%$

14 2012: 21% + 23% = 44%

2014: 25% + 27% = 52%

Difference = 8%

8% of 215 = 0.08 × 215 = 17.2 = 17 (to nearest whole person)

15 Class S interquartile range: 62 − 45 = 17

Class W interquartile range: 69 − 40 = 29

Difference = 29 − 17 = 12

16 2012:

Level 4 and above = 51% + 5% = 56%

56% of 32 = 0.56 × 32 = 18

2014:

Level 4 and above = 63% + 6% = 69%

69% of 28 = 0.69 × 28 = 19

Difference = 19 − 18 = 1

Numeracy practice paper 3

Mental arithmetic questions

1 15:315 = 3:63 = 1:21

2 0.005 ungraded

1 − 0.005 = 0.995 achieved a grade

$\dfrac{0.995}{0.005} = \dfrac{995}{5} = 199$

3 30 × €20 = €600

€600 = 600 × £0.80 = £480

4 40 × £8.50 = £340

10% of £340 = £34

£340 − £34 = £306

5 3 + 4 = 7

$\dfrac{£1764}{7} = £252$

£252 × 4 = £1008

6 12% of 84 = 0.12 × 84 = 10.08 = 10 (to the nearest whole number)

84 − 10 = 74

7 5 × 1 hr 5 mins = 5 hrs + 25 mins

Day is 7 hours long.

7 hrs − 5 hrs 25 mins = 1 hr 35 mins

8 38 × 6 = 228; 228 × £9 = £2052

9 Time taken (hrs) = distance (miles)/speed (mph)

$= \dfrac{60}{45} = \dfrac{4}{3} = 1\dfrac{1}{4}$

$1\dfrac{1}{3}$ hrs = 1 hr 20 mins

10 $\dfrac{4}{9}$ are male; $\dfrac{5}{9}$ are female

$\dfrac{5}{9}$ of 63 = 5 × 7 = 35

11 £425 out of £675 = $\dfrac{425}{675} = \dfrac{17}{27}$

12 52 × £5.50 = £286

Onscreen questions

1 Starting 15 mins earlier and ending 5 mins later adds 20 mins to each day. Reducing the break by 15 mins means net increase of 35 mins per day.

OR

Present school lesson time: 6 hrs 45 mins − 1 hr 30 mins = 5 hrs 15 mins

New time: 7 hrs 5 mins − 1 hr 15 mins = 5 hrs 50 mins

50 − 15 = 35

2 30 pupils achieved less than 40.

Total number taking the test = 108

108 − 30 = 78

3 0.5m² = 5000cm²

$\dfrac{5000}{625} = 8$

$\dfrac{30}{8}$ = 3.75 = 4 (rounded up to the next whole number)

4 Cost of additional miles:

45 × 65p = £29.25

$$\frac{35}{20} = 1 \text{ (rounded down)}$$

Only 1 free entrance

$35 - 1 = 34$

$34 \times £4.50 = £153$

Total cost:

$£250 + £29.25 + £153 = £432.25$

Cost per pupil = $\dfrac{£432.25}{35}$ = £12.35

5 Mean score = sum of two scores/2

The pupil with the highest mean score is the pupil with the highest score total.

Look at the two pupils who scored the highest in each test, and whose points are nearest to (100, 100).

(96, 85) has mean score of 90.5

(83, 91) has mean score of 87

No one else scored higher than 87 on either test, so no more calculations required.

6 $\dfrac{28}{35} = 0.8$

$\dfrac{14}{20} = 0.7$

$\dfrac{13}{30} = 0.433 \text{ (3 dp)}$

$\dfrac{23}{30} = 0.767 \text{ (3 dp)}$

$\dfrac{11}{15} = 0.733 \text{ (3 dp)}$

The answer has to be correct to 2 dp, so retain third dp in the working.

Total = 3.433

$\dfrac{3.433}{5} = 0.6866 = 0.69 \text{ (2 dp)}$

7 $\dfrac{4}{11}$ of £5654 = $\dfrac{4}{11} \times £5654 = £2056$

8 Length = 25m + 2 × 6m = 37m

Width = 16.5m + 2 × 6m = 28.5m

Area required: 37m × 28.5m = 1054.5m²

9 Statement A: The total number of pupils in Years 7 to 11 is 418.

Total number of pupils = 74 + 85 + 92 + 79 + 88 = 418

Statement A is true.

Statement B: The mean number of pupils per year group is 83 (to the nearest whole number).

$\dfrac{418}{5}$ = 83.6 = 84 (to the nearest whole number)

Statement B is not true.

Statement C: The median number of pupils per year group is 85.

In order: 74, 79, 85, 88, 92

Middlemost value = 85

Statement C is true.

Statement D: Approximately 21% of the pupils are in Yvear 11.

$\dfrac{88}{418}$ × 100% = 21.05%

Statement D is true.

10 In school:

24 × 0.7 = 17

22 × 0.6 = 13

16 × 0.5 = 8

21 × 0.3 = 6

28 × 0.6 = 17

24 × 0.25 = 6

17 × 0.4 = 7

Total number in school = 17 + 13 + 8 + 6 + 17 + 6 + 7 = 74

11 Total number of minutes = 4 + 3 + 5 + 2 + 9 + 4 = 27

Total number of secs = 26 + 52 + 25 + 55 + 29 + 17 = 204

$\dfrac{27\,\text{mins}}{6}$ = 4.5 mins = 4 mins 30 secs

$\dfrac{204\,\text{mins}}{6}$ = 34 secs

4 mins 30 secs + 34 secs = 5 mins 4 secs

12 2014 interquartile range: 69 − 42 = 27

2012 interquartile range: 65 − 35 = 30

Difference = 3

13 Total number of laps:

$(1 \times 3) + (2 \times 26) + (3 \times 48) + (4 \times 36) + (5 \times 28) + (6 \times 10) + (7 \times 1) = 550$

Total distance:

$550 \times 400m = 220,000m = 220km$

14 Total number of pupils = $3 + 26 + 48 + 36 + 28 + 10 + 1 = 152$

Median is mean of pupils 76/77

Cumulative frequencies are

Laps	Pupils	Cum Freq
1	3	3
2	26	29
3	48	77
4	36	
5	28	
6	10	
7	1	

Median pupils (76/77) fall into the category of 3 laps

15 59.4% of 2643 = $0.594 \times 2643 = 1569.942 = 1570$ (to the nearest whole number)

16 Statement A: Fewer Year 8 children spend more than three hours playing computer games per day than Year 7 children.

More than 3 hrs:

Year 7: $0.15 \times 28 = 4.2$

Year 8: $0.3 \times 35 = 10.5$

$10.5 > 4.2$

Statement A is not true.

Statement B: More than 50% of the Year 8 pupils surveyed play computer games for more than two hours per day.

More than 2 hours/Year 8:

$35\% + 30\% = 65\% > 50\%$

Statement B is true.

Statement C: Of the Year 7 children surveyed, only 4 play computer games for less than one hour per day.

Less than one hour/Year 7:

15% of 28 = 0.15 × 28 = 4.2

Statement C is true.

Numeracy practice paper 4

Mental arithmetic questions

1   58.5m × 75m = 4387.5m^2

2 $\dfrac{£6525}{60}$ = £108.75

3 $\dfrac{14}{322} = \dfrac{2}{46} = \dfrac{1}{23}$

4   6.9m − 3.42m = 3.48m

5   Ratio M:F = 7:13

Proportion of males = $\dfrac{7}{(7+13)} = \dfrac{7}{20}$ = 0.35

6   3 + 4.5 + 5.7 = 13.2

$\dfrac{13.2\text{km}}{3}$ = 4.4km = 4km + 400m

7   30 × 20 × 15 = 600 × 15 = 9000

8   30 − 18 = 12

$\dfrac{12}{30}$ arrived on time

$\dfrac{12}{30}$ × 100% = 40%

9   0.78 achieved

100 − 78 = 22

0.22 did not achieve

$0.22 = \dfrac{22}{100} = \dfrac{11}{50}$

10   12 stone = 12 × 6.35kg = 76.2kg

11   76% of 120 = $\dfrac{76}{100}$ × 120 = 91.2 = 91 (to the nearest whole number)

12 $\dfrac{16}{20}$ × 100% = 80%

$\dfrac{18}{30}$ × 100% = 60%

$\dfrac{(80+60)\%}{2}$ = 70%

Onscreen questions

1 Substituting F = 79 in the formula:

$$\frac{5 \times (79 - 32)}{9} = \frac{5 \times 47}{9} = \frac{235}{9} = 26.11 = 26 \text{ (to the nearest whole number)}$$

2 4 and above:

6 + 1 + 8 + 3 = 18

Number of pupils:

2 + 4 + 9 + 6 + 1 + 1 + 3 + 5 + 8 + 3 = 42

Proportion:

$$\frac{18}{42} = \frac{3}{7}$$

3 Monday 15:30–17:30 = 2 hrs

2 hrs = 120 mins = 6 × 20 mins

Time for 6 appointments; 16 − 6 = 10 left to do.

Break 17:30–17:45

Monday 17:45–19:00 = 1 hr 15 min

1 hr 15 mins = 75 mins = 3 × 20 mins + 15 mins

Time for 3 appointments: 10 − 3 = 7 left to do.

Tuesday: 6 appointments before the break (same schedule as Monday) and final appointment at 17:45

Finish at 18:05

4 Test 3 has the lowest low mark and the lowest high mark.

5 Total number of observations = 10 + 8 + 14 + 9 = 41

Number graded as 'Good' = 5 + 3 + 5 + 2 = 15

$$\frac{15}{41} \times 100\% = 36.6\%$$

6 Cost of 45: 45 × £9.50 = £427.50

Cost of 50

15% discount means price is 0.85 × £9.50

50 × 0.85 × £9.50 = £403.75

Saving: £427.50 − £403.75 = £23.75

7   Pass score = 0.2A + 0.3B + 0.5C = 45

Substituting for parts A and B:

0.2 × 52 + 0.3 × 49 + 0.5C = 45

10.4 + 14.7 + 0.5C = 45

25.1 + 0.5C = 45

0.5C = 45 − 25.1 = 20.1

C = 40.2 = 40 (to the nearest whole number)

8   300 inches = 300 × 2.5cm = 750cm

290 inches = 290 × 2.5cm = 725cm

750cm × 725cm = 54,3750cm²

51m² = 510,000cm²

543,750 − 510,000 = 33,750cm²

9 $4\frac{3}{4}$ out of $21\frac{3}{4}$ = $\frac{4.75}{21.75}$ × 100% = 21.8 = 22 (to the nearest whole number)

10   Statement A: The card-making enterprise took the highest amount of money over the four weeks.

Card making: 32 + 56 + 65 + 43 = 196

Pot plants: 53 + 65 + 48 + 32 = 198

Badges: 44 + 35 + 69 + 65 = 213

196 < 198 < 213

Statement A is not true.

Statement B: The lowest sales were made by the pot-plant enterprise in week 4

Two lowest plotted points are card making (week 1) and pot plants (week 4)

Statement B is not true.

Statement C: The range of sales totals is £37.

Range = £69 − £32 = £37

Statement C is true.

Statement D: The mean sales total of the badge-making group is £50.58

$\frac{£213}{4}$ = £53.25

Statement D is not true.

11   210mm × 297mm = 21cm × 29.7cm = 623.7cm²

12   Boys: $\dfrac{(1.1+0.9+-2.5+-0.2)}{4} = \dfrac{-0.7}{4} = -0.2$ (1 dp)

Girls: $\dfrac{(0.4+1.2+0.6+1.8)}{4} = \dfrac{4.0}{4} = 1.0$

13   2013: 77.8 + 76.4 + 81.5 + 75.5 = 311.2

311.2/4 = 77.8

2014: 78.7 + 79.9 + 83.4 + 79.2 = 321.2

321.2/4 = 80.3

Difference: 80.3 − 77.8 = 2.5

14   2013: 18% of 76 = 0.18 × 76 = 13.68 = 14 (1 dp)

2014: 23% of 85 = 0.23 × 85 = 19.55 = 20 (1 dp)

Difference: 20 − 14 = 6

15   Increase: 28.5 − 26.4 = 2.1

$\dfrac{2.1}{26.4} \times 100\% = 7.95\% = 8.0\%$

16   £5 = €8; €1 = $£\dfrac{5}{8}$

Accommodation/meals:

€4400 = $4400 \times £\dfrac{5}{8}$ = £2750

$\dfrac{£2750}{20}$ = £137.50

Entry fees: $\dfrac{£580}{20}$ = £29

Sundries: $\dfrac{£675}{20}$ = £33.75

Spending money:

€50 = $50 \times £\dfrac{5}{8}$ = £31.25

Total cost per pupil = £137.50 + £75 + £29 + £33.75 + £31.25 = £306.50

Glossary

Accuracy: the degree of precision required, eg to the nearest whole number; requires rounding of the result of the calculation.

Age: actual age and reading age are measured in years and months. This may be written as year. month (where the dot is not a decimal point!) or year-month.

Algebra: the part of mathematics where letters are used instead of numbers.

Area: a measure of the space occupied by a two-dimensional shape, calculated by multiplying two lengths.

Average: a single value chosen or calculated to represent a group of values. See also *mean, median* and *mode*.

Bar chart: presents data as vertical or horizontal bars; the length of the bar indicates frequency of a data value.

Box and whisker diagram/plot: the 'whiskers' show the complete range of the data; the 'box' shows where half of the data lies (also called the interquartile range), the extent of which is established by identifying the upper quartile and the lower quartile.

Capacity: a measure of how much can fill a volume of space, measured in millilitres (ml), centilitres (cl) or litres (l).

Cohort: a group, eg of pupils, who share some common characteristic, eg who are studying German.

Consistently: following a trend over time with little change.

Conversion: process of changing from one currency to another, or from one number form to another (fraction, decimal, percentage), or from one unit to another (cm to m).

Correlation: a measure of the strength of a relationship between two variables; can be positive (one increases as the other increases) or negative (one increases as the other decreases); see diagram on page 76.

Cost: money amount calculated using the formula: cost = quantity × price.

Cumulative frequency: the total number of data items up to a given data value; can be plotted on a cumulative frequency curve which shows the number/proportion/percentage who, for example, scored up to a given value.

Decimal: numbers based on the denary number system; can have a decimal point, which indicates where the whole number part ends and the fractional part starts.

Denominator: bottom of a fraction.

Distance: a measure of length, usually measured in millimetres (mm), centimetres (cm), metres (m) or kilometres (km).

Distribution: the shape of the spread of data; the 'normal' distribution is a bell shape.

Exchange rate: information needed in order to convert an amount of money in one currency to an amount of money in another currency; usually given as a ratio.

Factor: of a whole number is another whole number that divides into it without a remainder.

Formula: a statement in words, or an equation using letters, to describe the relationship between two or more variables.

Fraction: part of a whole, expressed as one number (numerator) divided by another (denominator).

Frequency: the number of times a data value occurs; see also *cumulative frequency*.

Graph: see *cumulative frequency curve, line graph* and *scatter graph*.

Greater than: symbolised by >, compares two quantities and identifies the bigger of the two.

Interquartile range: a measure of spread, representing the middle half of the data; the difference between the upper quartile and the lower quartile.

Less than: symbolised by <, compares two quantities and identifies the smaller of the two.

Line graph: a visual representation of the relationship between two sets of related data; axes are labelled with the data being measured (eg scores against years). Points are plotted and a line drawn to join these points.

Lower quartile: the middlemost value of the bottom half of the data; marks the first 25% when data is arranged in ascending order.

Lowest terms: form of a fraction that cannot be divided – there is no common factor in the numerator and denominator. Also applies to ratios; the form for which there is no common factor for the two numbers.

Mean: an average; calculated by adding up all the values and then dividing by the number of values.

Measure: applies to money, time, length (or distance), area and volume.

Median: an average; the middlemost value when the values are arranged in order; for an even number of data values, the mean of the two middlemost values is used as the median.

Mode: an average, the value that occurs most frequently, ie with the highest frequency; the most popular.

Money: currency measured in £ (pounds sterling) in the United Kingdom, in € (euros) in the eurozone.

Numerator: top of a fraction.

Order of operations: the order in which, in the absence of brackets, a calculation should be carried out: multiply and divide first, then add and subtract.

Percentage: an amount measured out of 100; 30/10 = 30%; /100 represented by the % sign.

Percentage points: the amount, expressed as percentage, by which two percentages differ.

Percentile: when a data set is arranged in order and then divided into 100 parts, each part is a percentile; the first percentile is the value of the data item which marks the first $\frac{1}{100}$ of the data set.

Perimeter: the distance around a shape.

Pie chart: a method of presenting data; a circle cut into slices (from the centre to the circumference) with each sector of the circle representing a share of the total population.

Place value: the value of a digit, determined by its position within a number.

Population: in a survey, the group that is included in the data collection process.

Prediction: an estimate of future performance based on data from past event.

Proportion: the relationship between some part of a whole with the whole; usually expressed as a fraction, but can also be given as a percentage or as a decimal.

Quartiles: identify the quarter marks when the data is arranged in ascending order; see *lower quartile* and *upper quartile*.

Range: the difference between the highest and lowest values; gives a measure of the spread of the data.

Ratio: describes the relationship between two parts of a whole; expressed using the : sign.

Raw data: values as collected, prior to any production of statistics or presentation of the data in tabular form or using charts or other diagrams.

Rounding: adjusting the answer to a calculation to fit whatever level of accuracy is required; involves looking at the next digit and rounding up/down according to that digit. Depending on the context, it may be appropriate to round up or down, regardless of the place value of the digit to be rounded.

Scatter graph: compares two paired sets of data by recording, as a single point, each pair; each point represents, for example, one person.

Sector: part of a circle (a slice) created by two radii and the circumference between them.

Simplest form: see *lowest terms*.

Speed: the rate of change of position, measured for example in kilometres per hour.

Spread: a measure of how stretched or squeezed the data is in a distribution; also called dispersion.

Statistics: information derived from raw data.

Table: arrangements of rows and columns to present raw data in a concise fashion.

Time: measure involving seconds, minutes, hours, days, weeks and years.

Trend: when a line graph continues in a particular direction (upwards/downwards), this indicates a trend, eg of increasing scores, of decreasing numbers.

Two-way table: method of displaying raw data so as to compare two sets of data within a tabular format.

Upper quartile: the middlemost value of the top half of the data; marks position of 75% when data is arranged in ascending order.

Variable: data which varies, for example, over time or between people or tests or schools; examples include test scores or ages.

Volume: a measure of the space occupied by a three-dimensional shape, calculated by multiplying three lengths.

Weighting: a method of giving more credit to one test result than to another; usually expressed as a formula.

Whole number: a number with no fractional part.

Abbreviations and acronyms

ALIS	Advanced Level Information System		**LSCB**	Local Safeguarding Children Board
AO	assessment only		**m**	metre
cl	centilitre		**mm**	millimetre
cm	centimetre		**NCTL**	National College for Teaching and Leadership
CPD	continuing professional development			
cu in	cubic inches		**NEET**	not in education, employment or training
DfE	Department for Education		**NSPCC**	National Society for the Prevention of Cruelty to Children
dp	decimal place(s)			
EYFS	Early Years Foundation Stage		**NVQ**	National Vocational Qualification
FAQ	frequently asked question		**Ofsted**	Office for Standards in Education
GCSE	General Certificate of Secondary Education		**PC**	personal computer
			PGCE	post graduate certificate of education
HM	Her Majesty's		**QTS**	qualified teacher status
ITT	Initial Teacher Training		**RIS**	Researchers in Schools
km	kilometre		**SCITT**	school-centred initial teacher training
KS	Key Stage		**SEN**	special educational needs
l	litre		**SEP**	School Experience Programme
LA	local authority		**SKE**	subject knowledge enhancement

Index

Terms in **bold** are main topics from the Professional Skills Test specification.

Index